PRAISE FOR *AXIOMATIC*

"An explosion of a book. Plumbing the depths of injustice, trauma, prison, and the flaw of good intentions, Maria Tumarkin is an important voice on American shores. Her eye is razor-sharp, her writing unsparing."

—Mark Haber, Brazos Bookstore

"A stunning exploration of the ways grief and trauma live on inside both our communities and ourselves. *Axiomatic* seeks to explore how poorly equipped our self-made structures—both civic and emotional—are to deal with serious pain, and Tumarkin does so with a crystalline intelligence, submerging the reader into her own brightly lit consciousness."

—Vanessa Martini, City Lights Books

"As brilliant and idiosyncratic as writing gets. The topics Tumarkin addresses serve to ask a larger question: as we move through the world, how do we address the effect we have on one another? *Axiomatic* feels like the best conversation you've ever had with the smartest person you've ever met."

—Thomas Flynn, Volumes Bookcafe

"With penetrating sentences that feel as though they've each been sharpened to an individual point, Tumarkin excavates the origins of trauma in all its unknowable vastness and unwavering turpitude."

—Justin Walls, Powell's Books

"Tumarkin's profiles of courage, justice, and history are bolstered by quotes and passages from writers as distinct as Raymond Carver, Wisława Szymborska, and Julia Kristeva. With their help she finds the fittest words to explore her subjects and excavate memories, 'whole honeycombs of them.'"

—John Francisconi, Bank Square Books

"*Axiomatic* is a book I went into with high expectations that were absolutely met and surpassed on all levels."

—Hans Weyandt, Milkweed Books

"Does time really heal all wounds or only pass them on? In a series of case studies that shift the focus from the motives and humanity of the rescuer to those of the people needing help, Tumarkin's passionate and compassionate study of trauma explores what humans do with their pain and dramatically shows that there is no one-size-fits-all answer."

—Laurie Greer, Politics and Prose

"A raw and honest look at trauma without any excuses or pleas for pity. Everyone should be required to read this book, if for no other reason than to better understand those around us."

—Nick Buzanski, Book Culture

"The hybrid pieces—journalistic, essayistic, and autobiographical—in Tumarkin's *Axiomatic* feel daring, unsettling, revelatory. Her writing—with intense empathy, disciplined cultural history, and up-to-the-moment analysis—brings us all closer to truth."

—Arlo Klahr, Skylight Books

"Tumarkin shares with [Helen] Garner a gimlet eye for the flaws in official systems, along with a fascination for the narratives nested in everyday lives. *Axiomatic*'s symphonic structure, however, recalls Svetlana Alexievich, the Belarusian journalist and Nobel Laureate. She is another for whom reality attracts like a magnet, who has made a career out of appropriating and braiding voices and documents, seeing the world as a chorus and a collage. With this remarkable, wild, risk-laden book, Tumarkin has earned the right to be mentioned in the same breath as both of them."

—*The Saturday Paper*

"*Axiomatic* is a series of open-ended essays about different people, as well as Tumarkin's own intense experiences of love and friendship. Consoling pieties do not interest her. There is no resolution, no comfort. It is a bleak view of the world, but for many people, including Tumarkin's friend Vera, 'That's how it goes.' This happened. That happened. I am here. You are here. Lucky for us Tumarkin is here, too. Trying."

—*The Monthly*

"Again and again in *Axiomatic*, Tumarkin confronts the meagreness of the written word in the face of trauma as she muses on her inability to write the text she had intended. Yet again and again, she herself demonstrates what literary prose can do."

—*Sydney Morning Herald*

AXIOMATIC

AXIOMATIC

Maria Tumarkin

TRANSIT
BOOKS

Published by Transit Books
2301 Telegraph Avenue, Oakland, California 94612
www.transitbooks.org

Copyright © Maria Tumarkin, 2018

First US edition published by Transit Books in 2019

LIBRARY OF CONGRESS CONTROL NUMBER: 2019942973

DESIGN & TYPESETTING
Justin Carder

DISTRIBUTED BY
Consortium Book Sales & Distribution
(800) 283-3572 | cbsd.com

Printed in the United States of America

9 8 7 6 5 4 3 2 1

CONTENTS

Some names have been changed (Vanda's clients in 'History repeats itself') or turned into initials ('Time heals all wounds') or removed altogether ('Those who forget the past are condemned to re———'). This was done for reasons of privacy and safety.

TIME HEALS ALL WOUNDS

FOR FIVE YEARS everything Frances wrote was about her sister. Once she had been good at deadpan humour. Where'd that go, and the sarcasm? She was seventeen, Katie had been sixteen. Their mother used to deck them in matching clothes: denim dresses most often. People mistook them for twins.

In a Year 12 English assignment Frances wrote

when I walked into her room that morning I could sense something was terribly wrong. She was positioned awkwardly, defying gravity.

A year later at uni

kneeling forward on her knees, incredibly still. I thought she had fallen asleep, obliquely...

Part way through an end-of-semester piece the following year

hair was falling over her face, shielding the truth. Her body was covered in prominent blue veins, gripping themselves over her youthful body.

After five years something shifted. Questions—why'd she call and ask me to wake her? why would she want me to find her? and the big one: did she mean it?—were no longer at Frances's throat. Frances could imagine them turning into statements.

SHE WANTED ME TO FIND HER

SHE MEANT IT

Five more years and Frances doesn't need to talk about it that much, maybe to some people, maybe once in a while. She knows what movies to avoid and with her sisters they don't need to go over it. Maybe her father was wanting some family talk when he said 'Cheers to Katie' on the tenth anniversary and they all raised a glass? It's possible. She'll ask him.

I meet Frances as the shifting is beginning. Katie's death doesn't sit anymore on her chest at all times, making her work for every breath, its knees pressed into her ribs. I was so lost when you met me, she'll tell me later, so confused, and young, bound up all the way with her.

We meet and I ask Frances about casseroles. Everyone knows about casseroles. A person dies and people—close, dear people and virtual strangers, some signed up to a special roster—converge on the dead person's house bearing casseroles. And the way the casseroles appear and just as suddenly disappear, weeks later, brings to mind, it is true, flocks of birds swooping down then taking off. Swish. For those weeks, sometimes—though not frequently—months, the family inside that house, *whoever* is there inside the house, is entombed in an intense concentration of throbbing, desperate human attention. Then it stops. Which is worse is hard to know although people I speak to before speaking to Frances—people who once found themselves on the receiving end of casseroles—seem to prefer the post-casserole. On a tram along Elizabeth Street we talk about the weeks after Katie's death.

—*What* period? (she's thrown by my accent; the tram is noisy)

—Casserole period.

—Oh, loved it. Wish it continued, went on much longer. I wish we had the casserole period now.

All those people in the house and no room left for flowers felt to Frances like the opposite of being scorchingly alone. 'And then,' she says, 'the flowers died. And the people left. And there was nothing to fill the emptiness with.'

Frances's Year 12 creative writing assignment, handed in twenty days after Katie's suicide—

I will never forget the taste of her mouth. I can still taste her last breath.

Five hundred and fifty or so girls from prep to Year 12 is a small school. Ann taught there twenty-one years. She taught all four sisters. (There were four sisters once. 'Four is special, three is ordinary,' Frances says.) In a two-hour conversation Ann—composed, a teacher-teacher, tough, a mother of however many boys, retired now—gets visibly upset only once. Why can't she claw back her tears when talk goes to that year's creative writing assignments: the piece Frances wrote, and two pieces from other girls, one of them living in a psych unit, both in Frances's class? 'I suppose because I was privy to the truth. This is the stuff they don't tell their parents. Or friends, shrinks. It's stuff they only tell themselves.'

One of the things about coming to this world from the Eastern European elsewhere (not that it matters much which elsewhere the elsewhere is) is that words do not often feel powerful in the world of Australia we've come to. Which is fine really. We have made our peace with this, accepted it, with gratitude almost, because we judged the well-known (to us) alternative—a world in which poets and their families were persecuted and killed for their words mattering too much—to be an evil much greater.

But perhaps I was wrong about this new world. Looking in all the wrong places perhaps. I wasn't looking at girls and boys writing about what is innermost to them and what they have decided language cannot deal with and submitting their heartbeats as assignments, burying them among the mountains of straight, dashed-off bits of second-guessing fluff, this transaction bypassing the school economy of words-for-grades because what is being exchanged illicitly, covertly, are secrets and confidences and questions, and soul pain. And teachers carrying words by their students inside their chests—I was not looking at them. And no one else knows. Of course nobody knows. 'You say to the Year 11 kids,' says Ann, 'if you have a special, special thing to write about save it till Year 12. Then when you write about a truth, it comes through. And they do save it, most of them.'

Ann is short so learned to wear bright clothes back when she was a teacher at a boys' school. ('They won't see you, they'll just knock you over.') She learned to never teach sitting down. She learned that with certain kids you want to give them your mobile number no matter what the classroom protocols say; that you must take a student's word for it, even if you'll at times live to regret it; that—and this bit's the tricky/obvious—you cannot be afraid of the kids.

Frances remembers none of her final-year classes except for English classes with Ann.

That year they were studying *Look Both Ways*, a movie about how to live is to stumble on death and grief, directed by the late (not late then) Sarah Watt and starring her husband William McInnes. Someone at the school knew McInnes so he was invited to chat to the Year 12s. Then Katie died and it was too late to change the curriculum; the following year, the turn of Katie's year to do Year 12 English, they stayed right off *Look Both Ways*. After Katie's death Frances's class went silent. No one would discuss the movie. For the rest of that year Ann had to say all the words. She told Frances to leave class anytime she needed: get up, walk out, just stay on campus. But Frances would not leave. She would sit there, in front of Ann, tears pouring. Not moving. Ann would give her tissues. And keep teaching.

Monique in another Melbourne school lost a Year 11 boy she had been teaching since Year 7. Frances and Monique do not know each other. Ann doesn't know Monique. Monique didn't find Bryn's body. Another teacher rang to tell her. When that teacher rang again, seeking someone's phone number, six years later, for the first time since that other time, Monique's heart went straight to her throat. Ambushed by memory, that's how it felt. This is what Monique tells me about Bryn—he was school captain in junior school, 'pretty powerful individual', an only child, only grandchild, spent the first part of his life in Thailand around Buddhist monks. So clever he managed to say his goodbyes to everybody and put together a playlist for his funeral.

'Look at me, I'm in full school uniform' was the last thing Bryn said to Monique. She hadn't seen him in full uniform in three, four years. Not that Monique would care. But it was as if he had a things-to-do sheet. As if he was ticking things off. What was on the playlist? "Mad World"—Tears for Fears—

HELLO TEACHER TELL ME WHAT'S MY LESSON?

LOOK RIGHT THROUGH ME

I talk to Monique and she brings up casseroles. She says, I

am a funeral director's daughter, I should be one of those people who slip easily into death mode, I should be one of those people turning up at your house with casseroles. 'You have to ask yourself,' she says, 'what happens when the casseroles are gone? People's sympathy lasts two weeks, I reckon.' The world stops holding its breath for you. They all start living again and you can't. It should be obvious by now that Monique is not the casserole type. A couple of her friends lost family members and she sent flowers two weeks after everyone else.

Possible description of a human life: salad days at our peak, casserole days when it's over. And for those we leave behind, the post-casserole eternity.

Monique likes teenagers' company, their honesty. After Bryn's death she stood before his classmates not quite able to adjust her eyes on their faces. 'I cannot look at you because,' she said, 'I'll cry. I am as lost as you are. One thing I want to say, when we're at the funeral do not judge how other people react. Do not say they don't know him so they cannot grieve. Do not say they don't have a right to carry on.'

How hard it must be to grieve in a high school: everyone looking at everyone. Everyone, just about, is impossibly fragile. Friends hurt your heart more often and expertly than your enemies. Not inevitably, but pretty likely, there are cliques, hierarchies, inner circles, outer circles, circles within circles. A squabble broke out in Katie's year over who owns Katie now that she's dead, who has the right to be shattered in public. Also, who's in charge of organising laser-printed silver pendants with Katie's face on them from Chadstone shopping centre. And helium balloons, a letter strung to each, unloosed at a suburban beach. Frances remembers none of it. Has no memory of the funeral even, and she did get a high Year 12 score, that's fact, but has no idea, she says, how except—wait, it's not like it was yesterday she and you started talking (this book, your life: jinxed? a blowout?), think back.

A piece she wrote the year you met—

robots don't procrastinate, they don't have feelings, they are machines that are made to work.

'Can you give me a pen?' Frances's writings are spread out around us. I hand her a pen. She wants to drive my pen through the school and university assignments she has dutifully printed out (every one of them about Katie) for me. Wants to cross things out. She wants me to know that she knows all of this is bad writing. 'I am very aware of writing as a craft, I love technique, what works, what doesn't work. And these poems are shocking.'

After 'shocking' she says 'fake'. We get stuck into 'fake'. Wrong word maybe. What she is saying is she needed to protect Katie. She could not let people think her sister was selfish, or indifferent to others' suffering. Wanted them to know Katie was crushed by her boyfriend's suicide and could not bear being blamed. I say:

—When you think of the book you'll write one day, will it be non-fiction or will you fictionalise it?

—No, no, hate fiction. I got the worst marks in fiction. Lowest mark on my uni transcript. For me it's non-fiction all the way. So it's not simply a memoir I want to interweave deeper issues.

—Like?

—Like exploring the idea of family secrets. And relationships. How they change. I am interested in perspective shifts.

Voice shifts. Third person. First person. I have the title already: *What Katie Did Last.*

For a while I tell her of books others have written about their lost sisters and brothers, friends, kids. When we first meet these books are rare, semi-submerged, you have to have heard about them from someone and they have the power of revelation—so *there are* non-medico words to describe this and it does happen to families ('Looks like a functioning family, nice house, this is really strange,' a cop said after Katie died) *like them.* And Charles D'Ambrosio keeps his brother Danny's army surplus boots, the ones Danny died in, filled with rocks on his desk and John Niven, whose brother hanged himself, compares a suicide to a nuclear bomb because it 'entrains a chain reaction with an incredibly powerful half-life'. Then the books multiply in the culture. Till they, stories of suicide, seem to be everywhere. And it's in some ways good, some bad, and now Frances needs to protect herself—can't be stepping on hot coals every time you go get chicken stock at a supermarket—and I quit with my literary outreach.

It is not about her looking away. About choosing when to look.

I am not sure if writing her own book is still on the table.

In my childhood people said the best-looking kids come from mixed ethnicity. Frances is Eurasian. And beautiful, yes. If you don't mind I will leave it to you to visualise the skin, eyes, cheekbones, her hair. I didn't want to tell you straight away because something happens when we're told someone, a young woman especially, has a she'd-look-good-in-a-postage-bag league of beauty. We have been told little yet somehow we know now and are less alert, less hungry for something. Wrong to keep it from you much longer, though. Frances thought Katie was the most beautiful out of them all. How beautiful? Katie didn't need make-up, ever.

'Stunning, popular, unstoppable, involved in everything; she was extremely smart too,' says Frances, 'and funny. The entertainer. The leader.'

Bryn, says Monique, made friends with every wayward person. It was obvious after he died that he had been a shepherd for his school's lost kids.

• • •

The day after Katie's boyfriend killed himself—five weeks before she did—Katie spent the day at round 2 auditions for *Australian Idol*. She sang in its entirety the periodic table of the elements while doing backflips. She wasn't the least bit serious about getting in and getting on TV. Says Frances, 'She wanted to encourage science in the community.' Laughter in Frances's voice.

The boyfriend was technically an ex-boyfriend. They were together for about six months. He was older, no longer at school, didn't have a job, her parents did not approve. They didn't know about the drugs. The relationship was apparently intense. Friends remember fights followed by reiterations of love minutes later. Frances says Katie did not love him. 'When you are sixteen, who cares if it's real love, it's the drama.'

One May evening Katie and her boyfriend went to her Year 11 formal and Katie broke off the relationship afterwards. Shortly after that he killed himself. It became public knowledge that Katie on the phone was last to talk to him. The young man's family (though not his mother) blamed her. His older brother called her *murderer*. At the funeral Katie was not allowed to speak. No mention was made of their relationship, none of her, no space carved for her grief. His suicide smashed Katie. Straight after, she was put on suicide watch. Pre-breakup, it transpired, they had a pact and tried dying together. Katie told Frances she was not going to attempt it again. She said, 'I promise you as a sister.' Then she tried to hang herself in a school toilet. Someone disturbed her; she had to stop. 'It would have been absolutely appalling if she had done it at school,' says Ann. 'The ramifications. You can sell your house, move on, but you can't sell a school.'

At *Australian Idol* auditions the cameras were on Katie. Eight hours. Her entertaining crowds. A classmate remembers calling Katie: 'And she said "hi" and I said "are you at the auditions?" and she said "yeah, got through the first bit, going into the judges in a couple of hours" and I said "oh, yeah". And she's, like, "you know he died" and I'm like "yeah, we got told this morning" and I say "is everything OK?" and she is like "oh. Yeah." She must have been in absolute shock.'

Frances says, 'My sisters were my life. Four sisters: together. Four against the world.' Growing up, people mixing up her and Katie—she could never understand that. Now when she looks at childhood photos she sometimes struggles to pick the difference. Plus: the voice. 'I don't like hearing my voice played back because I sound like her, I feel it's her talking.' A glorious, true likeness bound all four. A friend from Katie's class remembers sister #2 (Frances is #3, Katie #4) entering the room at the funeral: 'We couldn't handle it. Like seeing a ghost.'

Something strange—'downright freaky' Frances says—

happened not long after. One of the regulars, a woman, at a cafe where Frances and Katie both worked had a job with Fremantle Media, the production company behind *Australian Idol*. That woman's brother killed himself sometime before Katie. When she found out about Katie the woman flew to Sydney and cut out each frame of Katie from eight hours of footage and sent the tape to Frances and the family. Frances watched the tape once then wouldn't touch it for five years. 'In that footage it wasn't HER. She's acting a bit crazy. She was just trying to get through the day.' Sister #1 (six years older than Frances) watched the tape every day that first year.

• • •

Bryn had no siblings but many friends and S had been his best mate since joining Bryn's school at the end of Year 7.

'Bryn's mother called with the news. Or his father. One of the parents. Sunday morning. I was in the kitchen having a cup of tea. There was this call and they said Bryn was found dead. Short conversation.'

In a little park under a big tree S and I talk quietly and, listening back on my mobile, the birds and the kids are louder than us.

S's parents were away. He called his grandmother. She came around. After that's a blur, especially the early weeks. He did not have to go to school but went. School was a good place to be. Friends and a couple of caring teachers were there. The only moment that whole year he felt let down and pissed off was the final assembly when the principal made no reference to Bryn. The following year Bryn's year were about to graduate and Monique got asked to speak at the valedictory dinner. 'I knew,' she says, 'by that time the school would have wanted it all to go away. And I hate public speaking. I got up. Big room with a lot of people in it. I said, the thing I am really good at is being in the right place at the right time, and I think I was in the right place right time when we lost Bryn. And the room went silent. And people were nodding. I knew I'd done right, in saying something.'

They were a special year, S says, unusually close. For the first few years afterwards a group would gather on Bryn's birthday. Sometimes out bush at a place his ashes were scattered they'd hold a picnic, talk about Bryn, be together. 'I said to the kids: we are different, we have had our hearts broken, we will never do it to anyone,' Monique tells me, 'remember this feeling.'

S teaches high-school English and humanities. 'I haven't thought much about the connection between Bryn's death and my decision to become a teacher.' I look at him disbelievingly. 'I am just trying to make myself,' he says, 'approachable. Make it easy for students to come and talk. Make myself available.' I don't press the point. It is enough that he is there and that he knows.

If kids ask Monique about a boy who killed himself years ago, she tells them. Say someone steps into the classroom and flippantly announces 'I just wanna kill myself'. Others'll whisper 'shhh, don't say it in front of her'. Students around her know.

Everywhere you look, you see holes—vacant chairs, empty desks, holes on class lists. Lockers: S's eyes used to bump against Bryn's locker all the time. Try to forget, how can you forget?

Yet no space for a suicide in a school's institutional memory existed. If the student were school captain, maybe they'd lay a plaque or something equally inconspicuous. With no allusion to cause of death. One school I know grew a rose garden at the parents' insistence. A rose garden floating in schoolgrounds, no explanation of its reason for being, a silent, fragrant signifier.

• • •

'Lisa,' I say—it was Lisa I talked to first about schools losing their kids, about wanting to write about it, by now we're friends—'is suicide the worst that can happen to a school?'

'School is an institution but it is like a family,' she says. 'In loco parentis—in the place of a parent. When a suicide happens a school is damaged irrevocably, like a family would be. A school is haunted by a suicide, like a family. Like a family you find yourself asking what didn't we do, didn't we see, should we have said, how?'

'Lisa, but how can a school keep safe young souls,' I say, 'that do not know themselves, do not know death is final, are in turmoil, often don't know to ask for help? Can any institution respond to such a demand?'

Lisa still teaches English and literature but not full time and no longer at Bryn's school. She paints, writes, plays in a band, looks fifteen years younger than she is supposed to. (No make-up like Katie.) She answers, 'In Raimond Gaita's book of essays is an excerpt from a letter by Anne Manne who tells her dear friend, Rai, that to really face up to the tragedy of his mother's suicide and a lifetime of its consequences he should find pity for himself as a young boy.'

Pity. I am struck by the word.

'A school should be able to find that pity,' says Lisa, 'for itself. That forgiveness.'

At home I pull down *After Romulus*, Gaita's book, and re-read him quoting from the letter then catching himself remembering something he once wrote: 'For the Greeks pity did not carry the connotations of condescension that it often does for us. It referred to a sorrowing compassion that is marked through and through by awe at our vulnerability to misfortune.' 'At this last school I heard about,' Monique says, 'the school captain killed himself the day before graduation. How'd they miss him? How did we miss Bryn?'

Pity and forgiveness, they are nothing like the booming, blaring, everywhere phrases: unbroken spirit, coming together, overcoming adversity, rebuilding, shared values, vision for the future. 'Community' feels wooden as something out of a grant application.

At Bryn's school, Stephen, a Year 10 boy, killed himself years before Bryn's suicide. Stood in front of a train at a nearby station. Not many people from Stephen's time remain at the school but Amanda, who taught Italian and got retrenched in pre-Bryn times, was there when the principal, dead now, gathered the Year 10s and said 'it's self-centred and indulgent of you to grieve. Think about Stephen's parents.'

Amanda's insides flipped when she heard that. Out of these kids being told they were selfish to feel anything, some were Stephen's friends and others had bullied him, called him a mad dog on the train platform on the way home the night before he killed himself.

'I had to go to a station. Stand on the platform. And think, what must you feel like to do that? Had to watch a train coming,' Amanda says. 'Try to exorcise this awful image that was in my head.'

Back in the classroom she spoke. 'This is not my place but I must tell you—of course you feel. You have every right to feel.' She went up to the principal, said it was wrong what he said. How that old principal hated her guts. Later he'd get rid of her but this once he couldn't deny her. He regathered the Year 10s. Said 'I made a mistake.' Feelings were allowed.

When Bryn ended his life a new principal was in place and unafraid of feelings: his own, others'. Teachers in tute rooms read aloud a factual non-euphemistic statement about what happened. Lisa, who was there, thinks it helped. No one afterwards was roaming the schoolyard wondering why pockets of distressed kids were crying. Lisa credits the old principal—a dinosaur who came to see and to disown parts of his dinosaur upbringing—for the turnaround. And outside the school's gates the culture was shifting too. Not like a bit of taboo erosion each year. Things were going in bursts and bounds. An Australian schools guide edited by psychologist Mardie Whitla sawed suicide away from the generic tragedies-slash-crises pile. Suicide was its own crisis, got its own chapter. Whitla's book was forward-thinking for its time. *Its time*—2003—in this story each year counts. For schools something bigger than institutional self-preservation was at stake. Still-developing teenage brains, no impulse control, peer pressure, suicide pacts, danger of clusters and contagion, romantic notions of death—what other institution had to contend with such a fusion? Each of these was real. What you got when you mixed them was real. 'Can't pretend nothing happened,' Mardie Whitla tells me.

'Principal needs to take charge. Parents need to know what school is planning to do.' Parents of the living, she means.

A tilt away from secrecy. From every school feeling on its own, besieged, so anxious about being destabilised by its students' feelings running amok—this being particularly the case in expensive private schools—that a principal of conservative bent might reckon himself justified in lambasting kids for not sitting tighter on their self-centred emotions. Then when Katie died, it was during a feelings-are-OK strange period of transition, when a suicide was no longer a stain on a school to be covered with both hands, more like a scar, a hurting rather than a tarnishing, and Bryn's death too, though it happened some years earlier, came in that time of reluctant tending-to not (frenetic) scrubbing-off. Grief was legitimate. It required, though, 'managing'.

This 'managing' thread ran all through federal health department guidelines issued three years after Whitla's book, and, looking back at the early 21st-century language—all the *schools should facilitate appropriate participation in expressions of condolence BUT* and other constipated tangles—it is plain how saturated it was with unease about the chance of suicide contagion. And scared: of protracted grief.

(And re how grief was to be managed, let's see: channelled into a renewed understanding of the preciousness of human life. Countered by school routines. Given validation but no room to expand or to assert its non-transience. Counselling—yes. Flags at half mast, shrines, special concerts, photos of the dead student stuck on walls—no.) The aftermath of a suicide was like a flash of some other world of humans without skin, and needed to be gone in a flash too.

Possible to start your education in a school of whispers and rumours, graduate from a school of full disclosure, and enter a world where the news headline suicide survival stories must be told says Australian mental health chief does not feel one bit eye-popping.

Most important in the new-world guidelines is this, 'Suicide should not be made into a prohibited topic, students must be allowed to talk.' Some things in the guidelines, 'Do not provide details of the method of suicide or attempted suicide,' are as they always were.

After a suicide a school may desperately want to do right, whatever right looks like, for the students most affected but its duty of care is to all students and by extension their families. Lisa estimates 10 to 15% of the student population after Bryn's death were devastated; the rest were shocked but not shocked to their core and 'kind of able to put it to one side'. Tension between duty of care to the 15% and the 85% will probably always be there. Such tension may just be defining of school as an institution. Always the 15% need different things than the 85% and neither are the needs of those 85% by any means uniform and all the while teachers are already giving their 100% and...

A number of kids in Amanda's Italian class were struggling with family illnesses. Stephen's suicide pushed everyone to the brink. Amanda walked in on a fight. This was when teachers speaking to students about what happened, teachers making themselves night-and-day available to kids they saw gasping for air because they considered it immoral to outsource this talking to the especially trained special specialists, were risking their jobs. She walked in and a boy whose mum was dying was dangling a chair above his head. Amanda took the boy out of the classroom. 'He fell on me and started crying.' She said nothing, only hugged him, went back inside. 'Look, we have to deal with it,' she said to the class. 'Don't tell anyone but if by the end of the year you can order a pizza, a limonata and a gelato, I'll pass you.'

Another boy in that class had lost his sister.

'What do you want?' Amanda asked him.

'I want them to talk to me.' Since his sister died people had been avoiding him with their eyes.

'Would you be prepared to answer their questions?'

Amanda put him in front of the class. For the rest of that year all they did was talk.

Amanda, many suitably qualified people would take you to task, they'd say: 'Did counsellors advise you on your radical course of action?' No. 'Did you do follow-up ensuring each individual student got long-term psychological aid? Did you involve family and other teachers? Did you consider the implications of students missing out on regular educational experiences and outcomes?'

No. No. NO; you were alone without help and these kids were turning insane with the pain they felt inside themselves and in each other's stomachs (where does pain live?) and you couldn't pretend. Who would be the first to throw a stone at you, Amanda?

A friend teaching in outer Melbourne lost a student recently, a fourteen-year-old named Lachlan:

> I was itching to get aggro, to tell the kids you only have one life, not three like the heroes in the video games you play—I wanted them to sign a contract. But teachers

were blocked off from being there for the kids. Yet the kids were itching to speak. School was bringing in counsellors. What were they going to do? They didn't know the kids. Didn't know Lachlan. They were saying it was mental health. I think there's more to it. On his Facebook page he wrote how he didn't suffer the problem you're meant to have starting high school—of leaving your friends behind—as he had no friends in primary school. And there were 150 comments underneath because so many kids could relate to friendlessness.

When a school goes into shutdown mode—it happens still, every unhappy school will always be unhappy in its own way (OR: only happy schools are alike)—it both closes in on itself and becomes overreliant on outsiders. On counsellors, experts. Gets scared to let students and teachers talk to each other. But stopping them? It doesn't work. Doesn't work, doesn't, although it would be a mistake to grow too confident that we know what does. Where to start with prevention, for instance?

Dear children, understand this, a lot of the time death is senseless.

Dear children, some of you will find within yourself great reserves of rage and sadness.

Dear children, the adults around you, your bastions of safety, are barely keeping it together.

Dear children, don't worry too much about strangers or terrorists hurting or killing you, statistically and by every other measure your biggest problem is your family.

I have spoken to parents disturbed or worse by their kids being dragged into well-meaning, externally mandated, class-wide, school-wide prevention-of-something programs in which students were told about the deaths or suffering of kids they had no connection with, then made to participate in rituals and activities that seemed senseless at best, the experience stirring in them not a heightened empathy or empowerment but niggling feelings of unease and foreboding. A melancholia. Or simply boredom.

One time a girl approached Amanda. 'Why talk to *me?*' Amanda was not fishing. She wanted to understand. 'Because,' the girl said, 'I thought you wouldn't be shocked.' What does it take to not be shocked? The girl was abused by a family member. Amanda thinks teachers should have the facts and stats laid down at teacher training. 'When I taught I knew the statistics,' Amanda says, 'of sexual abuse and every class I went into I'd say to myself: "Five in here, who are they?" Sometimes you can see them straightaway those five. I used to say to new teachers, do you know the statistics? How come no one teaches you any of it?'

S says none of it was part of his training.

Actually I must take it further—schools, despite their sincerely pursued, these days, aim of keeping students out of harm's way are structurally unable to do so 100%. Nature of the beast. The nature of human nature. Nature of adolescence and of sticking teenagers en masse into an institution. Too many sardines in one tight-sealed tin with a hook-up lock. It is the thing about being young ('all character and no experience' as Inga Clendinnen memorably wrote) and not always recognising how violated feels, that thing of having no map of the territory or a half-decent torch. Something else: space between a student and teacher cannot be made totally non-dangerous.

Power over another is like that, it's alchemically malleable, and there is always a grey zone, a 0.5%, a 0.05%. Sex. Doesn't have to be about that. Coercion is often a wolf in sheep's cuddly clothing when you are young.

Amanda, I say, did everything after school feel like a walk in the park?

• • •

I was working on this book and a year passed, then two, and two more (I struggled in vain not to be tossed off course) and that whole time I remembered nothing about being the person who emphatically does not like schools. Then my kids reminded me. Mum, you hate schools. Oh, I thought, schools drive me crazy, how is it I forgot? Perhaps tragedy did something to a school, peeled back something I had never understood about it before.

In Ukraine I went to Number 36 school for eight years; when we came to Australia I tried out two Melbourne high schools. Not much to tell you other than I couldn't stand all three schools roughly the same. I won't pretend I love schools now. I don't. There's the compulsory attendance for years without horizon. Whiffs of the army: lining up, obsession with uniforms. Having to raise your hand for the toilet. Crossing quadrangles past groups discussing parties to which you are non-invited. Undercooked curriculums, or misguidedly over-cooked. First realisation of the unbridled rewards that con-formity and good looks bring. And for every Monique, Ann or Amanda, ten so-so teachers or ten you won't connect with. This is if things are good and safe, no gangs or psychopaths on training wheels running the show, no predatory teachers, no eager purveyors of racism or homophobia, no dealers offering ice and smack at corner discounts, no trolls who won't rest till their victims are rearranged in foetal positions in bedrooms or cutting strips off themselves.

Also in this mix is your 'internal age', as David Rakoff phrased it—me, I may have been fifteen calendar-wise coming to Australia but felt more like thirty-nine on the inside, still decades away from that state of bliss defined by Rakoff as 'when your outside and inside are in sync, and soma and psyche mesh as perfectly as they're ever going to'. (Cancer got Rakoff at forty-seven. His own internal age? Between forty-seven and fifty-three, he reckoned.) Some people, possibly many people, are really good at being children. Me: nup. Nothing particularly awful happened. Just: powerlessness, choicelessness, dependency, always having to do things on someone else's terms. I couldn't wait for it to be over. It's over. I am goosewalking into my middle age (I almost typed Middle Ages) and it's my son's turn now (my daughter is done) and then, gods willing, it'll be their children. Watching them is its own torture.

Frances hated *leaving* school. It was her undergraduate years that were horrible. Back at school she'd felt supported, safe, surrounded by people who knew her and cared, then at uni kids were getting drunk and partying with abandon. She felt she had done all that before—before Katie. Three years at university, Frances did not make a friend. Later she did a Masters, that was better, she found people she could relate to. I say, I felt so alone too during my undergrad degree. I don't tell her about the loneliness of my school years.

• • •

If a teacher says, 'Today we shall talk about Antigone' (it happened to Frances)—could you take any of it seriously when your sister hung herself the other month? Or maybe it is in the face of death that school might make the greatest sense.

Mildura Secondary College—population 800—lost six kids and threw open its doors to everyone other than camera-wielding scum (scum is the image imprinted in people's memories of the media hangers-around). A stationwagon rounding a bend had ploughed into a straggle of teenagers. Barb, a teacher I know, visited one of the survivors in hospital and embedded in this girl's backside were ninety-six pieces of gravel that she later kept in a jar. The students were walking along the side of the road to a party.

The tragedy happened on a Saturday. All the area's schools made a big deal about Monday being a school day. Former students, friends from other schools, parents of the students who died were encouraged to come that Monday. The school's cafeteria was converted into a grieving room. The school helped arrange funerals for the kids whose families had no strong church links. The school's chaplain led the ceremonies. In the weeks and months following the death of Shane, Abby, Stevie-Lee, Cassandra, Cory and Josephine, the school became the crumbling world's centre—the centre that could hold. It was 2006. Years afterwards, it is as if something is caught in Barb's words, a fleck, timelessness.

I think of the off-duty nurses who rang each other, got

their kids minded, then went into the hospital that night to help wash the bodies before the families saw them. I think of how, as teachers, we faced the rest of the kids that first Monday morning and read the rolls, the names of the children we had lost still there. I think of the media and how ruthless they were and my boss striding across the oval telling cameramen to get off our grounds. I think of how happy I was we had such a large playground and the kids could grieve in private behind the big buildings.

'A week later, or a bit more, I came to school, got out of my car,' Barb says, 'and the school was noisy again. The most beautiful sound. Like birds coming back from the northern winter.'

Practice exams, actual exams, parent-teacher interviews, classes, things absurd in their random and stiff irrelevance, may re-emerge as shockproof, and important.

Start time of Japan's 2011 earthquake-tsunami-nuclear meltdown: 2.46 p.m. Most of the country's school-aged children were at … [obvious]. What's little realised is how much schools, in this natural and human-made disaster, sheltered the affected population. School gyms became relief distribution points. School walls were message boards. Many students seized control of apportioning food and medicine, and this granted them purpose, and structure. Eventually schools resumed being schools and students were transformed yet again. An Ishinomaki city principal said he never grasped what education could do until he saw children turn away from the debris and re-immerse in their school lives—and when Julie Pozzoli, eight weeks into the job as principal of Innisfail State High in north Queensland, saw her school reduced to ruins by category-five cyclone Larry she sensed her priority was to fling the gates back open. Because 'we had children needing to come to school. We needed to make things as normal as possible for them.' What a ubiquitous phrase it is—back to normal—but perhaps not as glib, nor so obscurantist, as it sounds. A local school can hold things together the way the medieval town square used to. As long as it was there, intact, the rest of a community could be reimagined around it.

'We were asked to maintain,' Barb tells me, 'a certain equilibrium, a certain peacefulness. Not peacefulness. A calm. We really tried. We just kept running classes. We were conscious not to sob in front of kids because there was enough sobbing.' Hardest was the grieving room's dismantling after the last funeral. Messages and poems from that room were wrapped in little packages for the parents to come and collect. The six lockers were not used for the rest of the year. Flowers, notes, decorations were stripped off them and the lockers left empty, untouched. Same with Katie's locker. Difficult to take the grieving room closure, says Barb, the school was flicking the switch back on and students and teachers went looking for ways of remembering the six. 'We kept the kids with us, on our arms'—armbands, made of rubber, yellow and blue of the school's colours. Some students wore them for two years without ever taking them off. Barb says sometimes with all that was going on, pain and loss, yes, also court hearings, an inquest, media reports, the incessant picking at the scabs—'It was almost a relief to go and be a teacher.'

Just as the culture is shifting but it's unclear where it's going Frances and I attend a forum on responses to suicide. We sit in the front row, notepads and pens on our knees, waiting, Frances whispering.

—Do you believe in PTSD?

—Not that much.

Onstage is a mix of historians, artists, academics, mental health workers, journalists, people who know what it is to be driven to suicide, others familiar with how getting left behind feels. They are the proof change is happening, language emerging. A good night, we agree, waiting for a tram afterwards. Frances says:

—I was infuriated, though. So angry. One of the media guys, that journalist, didn't you find him annoying? Didn't you see how special he felt breaking his youth suicide story, such a hero, and how very traumatised? Did you notice how fascinated he was with these young people's suicide? How drawn to it?

—I found him a bit narcissistic. He seemed to admire the depth of his own emotional response.

—Narcissistic that's right.

Reporting youth suicide was once considered akin to starting a fire and walking away from the scene of the arson, and journalists didn't do it. When *Four Corners* aired, in 2006, a sober and painstakingly researched look at the aftermath of seventeen-year-old Campbell Bolton's jump off a hotel roof, the show's EP Bruce Belsham spoke of grappling with the toughest set of editorial judgments of his career—more fraught than crystal meth, sex slavery, domestic terrorist recruitment and Australians on death row in Bali, all the stuff of *Four Corners* episodes that year alone. Later depression awareness group beyondblue successfully stopped a *60 Minutes* segment on four suicides in one Geelong school. In 2009. The argument? Same argument waged so long and backed by such thick sheafs of research I need only key in buzzwords—irresponsible/danger-ous/copycat/clusters.

Then one Monday night it was 2012. *Four Corners* covered a suicide cluster—twelve schoolkids; they were putting them-selves in front of trains, mostly—in outer Melbourne suburbia. In Albury-Wodonga the *Border Mail* ran four months of front-page youth suicide stories. By accident I had the TV on when the editor and staff were called up to receive a Walkley award for their campaign END SUICIDE SILENCE. The camera caught them swaying back and forth in the rhythmic, pain-releasing way people sometimes sway at funerals.

One of society's last silences goes crack like a ripe walnut? Or, more boringly, the offline world playing catch-up to peo-ple's online existences?

Another night: on my TV screen's a talk show, tonight's topic grief and time limits, and people with broad Australian accents and no special expertise in trauma are saying what great works of art have been saying for close to ever. They are saying stuff we've wilfully forgotten these last hundred or so years. 'This is not an illness. I'm not going to get over it. I'm going to live with it'—(mother of a deceased girl).

What I want to say, it'd be disingenuous of me not to shout it, is don't forget that this resurgent openness, fear's absence, is so new you can smell the factory paint on it.

Attempted, fantasised about. Considered, completed (creepy technical term), mourned, memorialised. On social media platforms suicide has been discussed since year dot, death (along with desire) being one of two great forces, as Sig-mund Freud knew, of human life and so they flow like two megarivers, death and sex, the Nile and the Amazon of the online world.

Bryn and Katie belong to this era's dawn. Not a trace of Bryn's life or death exists on the web; of Katie there is only her MySpace account, lingering on, which was where Frances found her suicide note a week after her death and where those who consider themselves Katie's friends used to post fluffy messages on her birthday and assorted other occasions despite her being dead, e.g.

> Happy Birthday Katie. It's been too long without seeing you Katie. I hope ur in the french exam room with me today!! U were always better at French, especially those poems ☺. Hope you're happy wherever you're. I was on placement and this girl from uni reminds me sooo much of u.

Is the banality touching? How much of this talking to Katie is self-gratifying, a performance: of cutesy, naive disregard for the finality of her death? A not-swallowing of its irreversibleness. Katie this, Katie that. I hear a coroner—she examines young bodies—say young people do not get *finality*. Once dead, you stay dead, how to teach that—that some things can't be deleted, undone, when pretty much everything at that age is trial and error? Perhaps pray for error. A mother of a teenager who died under a train remembered her daughter's friends kept calling and texting her dead daughter's smartphone, as if the phone were a portal, connecting them to the underworld, or as if the phone could be a replacement for her vanished body (like wafer to the body of Christ), unless what they were sensing was the phone was with her. In that place where the battery would not go flat.

Katie after her boyfriend killed himself posted messages to his MySpace account. She direct-addressed him too. *You didn't wait for me. I will see you very soon*—this is what a friend remembers Katie's posts saying.

'There might be more bullying on Facebook but Facebook is all white and upfront, MySpace was dark,' Monique says.

I like this thought from Stacey Pitsillides. When the future's archaeologists search for 21st-century traces 'what they will find on the internet will resemble what they find under the ground: mainly garbage and graves'.

In online condolence books it's the dead who are spoken to, not, as tradition once dictated, the bereaved family. We in the West have long been doing our speaking to the dead in private; were we to do so with some regularity publicly, in the glittering sunlight of day, we'd risk being diagnosed with complicated grief disorder or worse. Online, talking to the dead, sharing with them goings-on, letting them know how much they're missed, reminiscing, petitioning them for help, makes sense. The asynchronous, one-way, publicly visible style of the communication looks and feels natural. It's how people generally talk online. Facebook pages of the dead where these conversations play out are anything but the online world's kooky underbelly. In the words of Régine Debatty (curator, critic, blogger) they lie somewhere between 'the gravestone and that teenage bedroom that never gets touched'. Our rituals are changing and Debatty thinks in matters of grief, and not only, we are taking our cues from teenagers.

No place until recently in our Western anglophone culture

for overflowing, unpushawayable grief. Big grief. Long grief. No place for the grief of Demeter, who Ovid describes in *Metamorphoses*, the Greek goddess of earth, harvests and agriculture who grieved without rest for her daughter, Persephone, and 'reproached the whole wide world—ungrateful, not deserving her gift of grain'. She grieved and the world suffered. She grieved and earth went barren.

• • •

Oh, Katie, you sent the suicide note to your own MySpace account. This was before Facebook did to MySpace what Coke did to Pepsi and Frances says the message said—

Hi Frances, you're probably reading it and I'm probably dead blah blah. Miss you guys.

Were you giving yourself a chance to change your mind in the last moment?

I sit across from your sister in a nearly empty cafe that can comfortably gobble up half a dozen office Christmas parties, and watch tears jump off her cheekbones and fall on her neck. The tears feel endless even though they are not gushing out of her eyes but rolling quietly like beads. 'The number of times I cried is ridiculous,' Frances says. *Cried*, past tense, this coffee we're having is a fair few Christmas seasons ago. She looks ageless when crying, sister #3.

Exact iteration of last two sentences in the suicide note—

if ANYONE feels that this is their fault, tell them i say it

ISN'T. Even me, writing this letter, don't know if it's going to be read in the future or be deleted by me.

Katie, were you conjuring the world without you in it—or with you in it, only dead? Trying to speak from a place of no longer being here, while still alive?

From Frances's third-year undergrad creative writing assignment—

so many spelling and grammar mistakes, too, as if she went to little effort to write this note, as if she didn't think that anyone would read it or that she needed it.

Campbell Bolton's note, left on his bed, was long, thoughtful. 'Please do not assume you know why. Even I'm not completely sure. It is simply the best thing to do. The mechanism telling me not to kill myself is broken.'

Katie, your note was like a wave that just slipped out of you, too painful to write anything other? Or did you find that even though you had thought you wanted to be dead you couldn't take seriously the possibility of actually succeeding? Old Freud's dictum—'our unconscious does not believe in its own death; it behaves as if it were immortal.'

(Bryn's note was what might be called traditional. He said his goodbyes, made a point of wishing a special bye to his parents, and apologised to whoever would find him. To S he wrote, 'You are a great mate.')

• • •

S tells me:

—For a while I used to write letters to Bryn.

—Letters on paper?

—On paper. *This is what I've been thinking. This is what's been happening in my life.*

—What did you do with the letters?

—Write them then burn them.

In China to honour the dead they burn offerings made out of paper—paper money, houses, cars, clothes, paper versions of the latest blockbusters. They burn representations of stuff the dead may need in the afterlife. Of course the dead have needs, what's more they have standards, and you do not wish to disappoint. Katie died the week that the last Harry Potter book came out. 'My mum was, like, *she wouldn't even wait for Harry Potter.*' Frances is laugh/cry-ing now. 'I read the book all in one night and couldn't remember a thing.' Frances's mum is Chinese. Buddhist. She asked Frances to write Katie a note, put it in the book, burn it. The grandmother burned a little paper house. Frances burned *Harry Potter and the Deathly Hallows*, for her mum really, not for Katie. (In an interview J.K. Rowling said a crucial decision she made early on is that in her books magic cannot bring the dead back to life. Dead stay dead.)

'I know why we try to keep the dead alive,' writes Joan Didion in *The Year of Magical Thinking*, 'we try to keep them alive in order to keep them with us. I also know that if we are to live ourselves there comes a point at which we must relinquish the dead, let them go, keep them dead.'

Once a week a cleaner came. Frances's mum would hide all Katie photos, remove every signal of absence. Don't touch that room, she'd tell the cleaner, my youngest needs to learn to do it herself.

Tough love n'all.

you told me you did this because you didn't want the cleaner to know that someone had died in the house, but I knew it was because for three hours of every week you could pretend Katie was still alive. ('A Confession to My Mother', third-year creative writing)

Joan Didion could not give away her husband's shoes: if he came back he'd need them. The smartest people on the planet wait for the dead's return. Each night Frances lay awake. Her bedroom was next to Katie's old room. 'I'd make myself get up, go to the bathroom, walk past her room, feel that initial fear of finding her over and over again.' Frances would get up at least ten times a night—ten times nightly ten years ago, you understand. 'I didn't actually need to go to the toilet. And I was frightened to my sheer core.' As if she was punishing herself for not being there when her sister killed herself, or possibly seeking inoculation, try and wear out the demon through single-minded repetition. People called Frances stoic and she thought of herself as a coward. When finally she was asleep, dreams would come. In the dreams Katie was trying to hang herself from various places, often off a tree at a park near school to which Frances would run, desperate to save her sister, and to save others from seeing her sister dead. Sometimes in a dream Katie would come 'alive and sparkling' to Frances, and Frances would be filled with a euphoria unlike any she'd known.

'Grief turns out to be a place none of us know until we reach it'—Didion.

Grief made Frances see her parents as if for the first time. The time you realise that your parents are human, that they feel, and carry, incredible pain, it's an epiphany she says. Sight of her mother wailing on Katie's bed that morning...

when I saw you curled up on Katie's bed you reminded me of a whimpering infant, a helpless child, not the fierce mother you always were.

Hurt and loneliness of her father…

all he has is his children and his books. Books are treated with respect in our household. Bright shelves of great novelists lighten up our home and every page has felt the breath of my father.

(Ann read these lines out in Year 12 English class. Frances read them to her mum. Her mum doesn't usually read Frances's writing, she's not comfortable reading in English. She loved the bright shelves line, though.)

To get to sleep Frances would drift off to *Friends*, a show so intolerably twee now but a megahit, let's not forget, for the ten seasons it ran. 'After she died I watched all the *Friends* series. I had to fall asleep to *Friends* every single night for five years. Do you know how many times that means I watched each of those episodes? Because the voices drowned out my thoughts.' Turning *Friends* off was a massive step. After that dreams were still there but she could let go of the jamming device.

• • •

I am a mother of a young woman. My daughter has not been well in her soul (her body too) for a while now. I can't help it—can't help being scared shitless. Have read and watched interviews with parents of kids who killed themselves. Each parent is burnt out with shock. Each parent did not in darkest dreams dream they were the one walking behind the coffin. 'If someone like Chanelle does it, you just can't stop it,' said Karen Rae, her daughter's suicide the fourth in six months, same Geelong high school, 'because she was the last person in the world you would ever expect to do it.' *Last person in the world you would ever expect.* Can any parent listen to these words and have them whiz by, no sting? A father said, 'I thought there had to be dysfunction, like alcohol abuse, step-parents, child abuse... But then it happened to us.'

If this does not put fear of god in you what will?

Frances and Katie used to sneak out the house at night. The night before killing herself Katie was out till the pre-dawn hours. I speak to my daughter. She says, 'Oh, yeah, lots of people do that.'

While my daughter was still at school she'd say, 'Don't worry, mamochka. Our flat is too small and my window is too narrow.'

Then when we moved—she was an adult by then—by chance the window in her bedroom was the kind that didn't open.

I don't know how not to be scared and if it's important that I try—children and parents always lead double lives, this separateness, a mutual elusiveness, being something like a structural necessity and yes I knew when and where my daughter smoked (and how much she and her friends paid for) her first joint, so what? So nothing. Parts of us will always, must always, remain unknowable to each other.

Unknowability triples in the period between childhood and adulthood. This is when we carry out, often involuntarily, a program of inquiry 'into the nature and effects of mortality, entropy, heartbreak, violence, failure, cowardice, duplicity, cruelty, and grief; the researcher learns their histories, and their bitter lessons, by heart'. That is how American writer Michael Chabon (possibly relevant: a father of four) puts it—above and below—and it can't be improved. In the process of inquiry the researcher discovers

> the world has been broken for as long as anyone can remember, and struggles to reconcile this fact with the ache of cosmic nostalgia that arises, from time to time, in the researcher's heart: an intimation of vanished glory, of lost wholeness, a memory of the world unbroken. We call the moment at which this ache first arises 'adolescence'.

The ache of which Chabon writes tends to be treated as a developmental stage, like pooing into a nappy, devoid of far-reaching moral seriousness. When big thoughts and emotions of adolescence do get taken seriously the serious taking is usually done in the language of mental health.

Frances sends me a poem of Katie's she found in Katie's school diary—

> thoughts flood my head
> poisoning my mind,
> your slipping from my grasp
> leaving yourself behind.
> Shadows haunt my mood,
> guilt follows a laugh,
> my life used to be full
> it's now cut down to half.

In the diary, next to the date her boyfriend died, is *my boy said that he would never leave before me. he promised that he would always wait for me. he promised … promises ain't worth shit.*

When Melanie Woss's family approached Pan Macmillan to see if their daughter's work might be publishable, Fiona Giles was an editor there. When Fiona was thirteen her brother, seventeen, gassed himself. 'I kind of identified with my brother, to some extent,' Fiona tells me. 'I identified with Melanie'— Melanie went to school at Perth's Methodist Ladies' College, where she was an undeniably brilliant student and tried unsuccessfully to gas herself in the science labs. ('I taped my nose so I couldn't breathe and then I taped Bunsen burner tubing into my mouth. I turned on the gas and then just lay on the bench.') In 1989 shortly before her eighteenth birthday she did kill herself. Her book—the collected writings of Melanie Woss, compiled and edited by Fiona Giles—is proof Melanie could have become an excellent writer. That it was published in 1992, the time of literary (and all other frontiers) stepping around youth suicide, feels astonishing.

Fiona, after she lost her brother, suffered bad depression. In her preface to Melanie's book she quotes Julia Kristeva, and writes—'depression is less an illness than a language which needs to be understood'; it's a preface which is in no way safely scholarly, the book no cautionary tale, or showcase of precociousness, but respectful of Melanie's oneness, and lucidity, its landing on Fiona's desk was great luck.

Melanie did not wish to grow up. She was scared of leaving school. Adolescence frightened and exhausted her. 'In childhood I was cuddled and looked after, and in adulthood I will cuddle and look after, but here, in the middle, I seem to get the rough end of both the childhood and adulthood sticks.' She felt the adult world was failing the children. A letter to a former teacher about six months before she died went—

Can dead children talk to each other?

Is there a name for when you feel really sad and unhappy
and you can't cry, even though you want to?

Can a person be too smart? [...]

What makes a baby try to walk after it falls?

How do we know what is happening is actually happening?

Could I go mad and kill myself without meaning to?

'Bryn was a high achiever,' Monique says. 'Some of the
kids were angry. *How could Bryn do it to us, and be so calculating?*
That's him, A+ really.'

Brilliant kids, good at nearly everything, awash with friends,
their talents and achievements get noticed, acclaimed, often
they're from privileged families, are killing themselves.

Fiona's brother was school captain.

Frances believed Katie died because of undiagnosed depression. Believing this made Katie's death make sense and
gave Frances a language to talk in, to reflect in.

Katie's dad thinks it's the drugs that did it. Mum thinks it's
the boyfriend.

So much of adolescence, you cannot quite convey to yourself or others why you let things happen. It takes years, longer,
to work it out. Sex, being bullied or a bully, friendships, betray-
als, how far you might go to feel like you belong, all those experiences you did not object to, not loudly enough, not convinc-
ingly enough. Ashamed. Never discount shame's power or its
cockroach-like tendency for lingering on. American academic
Brené Brown studies shame, and high schools rise up all the
time in her research, so much so that Brown thinks of high

school as *the metaphor* for shame. My daughter reminds me one of adolescence's constants is not knowing what's happening inside you. And by extension not knowing what you're capable of. You are like a painting that's gone beyond the paper. Watching my daughter's not-knowing … my heart must have stopped a few times. How must it be for her, for them?

• • •

1.
I had a best friend growing up. Recently she told me how one day not long ago she decided to throw herself off a high-rise. She crossed the city (the city we'd shared and I left on the very Saturday she turned sixteen) and manoeuvred herself up on some anonymous building's ledge. Her head was covered with a scarf. She had nothing to live for. Then she saw a cat. The cat came towards her. There was something about the cat, a neediness, a look in its eyes, warmth of its body, *something*. Anyway it pulled her off the ledge.

In time Frances has come to believe Katie's death cannot be explained away. With someone so young it is not one thing, it's everything, squashed and smashed together each bit reacting with every other bit, all the bits, in that one particular moment and five minutes later it could have been a completely different story.

• • •

Boori Pryor, whose father is from the Birri-gubba nation, his mother is Kunggandji, wrote a book *Maybe Tomorrow* documenting the big bite suicide took out of his family. His brother Nick hanged himself when developers acquired, defiled, sold off their land. It hurt that much. Aboriginal suicide is said to be profoundly existential. It is filled with meaning. It may be a demand for a respect one is not daily afforded, or asserting autonomy in a life marked by powerlessness. It could be a statement of anger. Perpetual cycles of grief may encircle it. It may be driven by loss of culture, an emptiness within. In the background: pounding of racism, of alienation. It may be a rational response to life (life = a situation too awful).

Another brother, Paul, couldn't handle being a black man—a successful black man: actor, storyteller—in a white world. Their sister Kimmy could find 'no space to breathe any fresh air into her body'. She was an artist. Had felt haunted, hunted, by shadows. 'It is impossible, unreasonable and immoral,' Colin Tatz writes in his *Aboriginal Suicide is Different*, 'to maintain "mental illness" as the key causation in Aboriginal suicide.'

Untreated depression or other mental illness is reckoned to be linked to nine-tenths of suicides in Australia right now and if you accept the model the solution is this: earlier diagnosis, more mental health services, greater mental health issues awareness. Lives have been saved. Families, saved. Still people are falling through cracks, no services in some areas, waits of months for an appointment, follow-through funding shortfalls. What is needed is more, of money, of services, more, if you accept the model.

I talk to Erminia Colucci, the fastest talker I know, who has studied attitudes to suicide and suicidal thoughts among young people in Italy, Australia, India. (There are intellectually rigorous reasons for her choice of countries. There are lovely, simple ones too: 'I am Italian. I love Australia. I am fascinated by India.') She noticed Australians use depression and mental health as explanations much more readily than Indians or Italians do. Why, I wonder. 'It's a Western framework,' Erminia says. 'Actually'—she stops herself—'the concept of the West is full of holes. Does Italy belong to the West? What I mean is it's an anglo way of looking at suicide.' Erminia's view of suicide is existential. You cannot begin to grapple with the SOMETHING-NESS of a suicide without talking about the crisis of meaning people experience, the what's-the-point-of-it-all questions that get asked and stay painfully unanswered.

It is not like anglo ways do not recognise soul. Our culture gets how what David Foster Wallace called The Bad Thing is much as Jenny Diski fixed it to paper. 'Place that makes no sense, that no sense can be made of, but which is all there is when I am in it … obscurity and obstacle always increasing.' It's just that when talking about suicide takes in culture, chemistry, disease, meaning, soul—'Conversation about suicide becomes almost unmanageable,' Erminia says.

Mental health is people's way of holding the conversation down like an animal.

'The concept of mental health,' Erminia thinks, 'is not a law. Not a religion, not a dogma.'

There can be no totalitarian theories about depression, mental health, suicide, human nature.

Easy to overlook, in the medicalised air, how much sorrow and pain about the world a person can carry inside. Your life may be privileged, safe, white but that won't make you immune from despair at the world. Doesn't mean you don't feel things with an intensity that turns being in the everyday—to-do lists, plans—excruciating at least some of the time. Fiona's brother grew up during war in Vietnam. Terrified he'd get called up. His family were antiwar campaigners. To him the wide world outside his window felt broken. Bryn was deeply sorrowful too for the world's state. 'It was the time,' S says, 'of the Iraq invasion.'

Frances says she won't read the draft of this chapter to the end. Too emotional: her words. Not gripped anymore by need-to-know is what she means I think.

PTSD, tram platform, that forum, the narcissist—'I was so angry' (Frances [then]).

Me (then) making notes—*People in pain's anger is clarifying, takes us closer to truth, rages at euphemistic bullshit, fixes contempt on those getting off on the high emotions around a young person's death.* Felt insightful that night, feels obvious now.

The five stages of thought, from the initial thwack to gah.

'Well, people are angry, aren't they?' says my friend Wendy, fresh back from seeing parents' angrily inconvenienced faces at a morning tea held for the dead (it was suicide) school captain at a sister school of her daughter's school. 'They are angry when traffic stops on the West Gate Bridge because someone has jumped off it. They are angry when trains get cancelled because someone leapt in front of one.'

Frances says she read an earlier version of the chapter and—Maria, it's fine, your interpretation. Anyway.

Everything has its limit including sorrow

No, not sorrow, it has no limit.

A camel sniffs at the rail with a resentful nostril;
a perspective cuts emptiness deep and even.
And what is space anyway if not the
body's absence at every given point?
(Joseph Brodsky.)

If life goes on does it follow that sooner or later the radius of pain starts shrinking and time will act as the disinfectant to people's wounds, as the warm water to bathe them in, as the large cotton towel with which people may make their wounds dry?

Amanda's brother's best friend shot himself one weekend. Amanda was sixteen. She says she's learned by now no *I'm over it* moment's going to come, that's that.

While Fiona was editing Melanie's book her father—long since divorced from her mother, married to another woman—drove his car into a tree.

Wendy thinks any kind of reckoning with a suicide can only happen 'after the casseroles stop'.

'We've had a million go on and become scientists and architects and I won't remember most,' Monique says. 'Maybe I'll remember a president. But I'll always remember the ones we lost.'

Mark Costello said of his close friend and one-time flat-mate David Foster Wallace, 'There was not enough velcro to keep Dave on this planet.'

Jean Améry said the only ethical stance is 'to revolt against the disappearance of the past in the biological dimension of time'. Améry, survivor of Auschwitz, Buchenwald, Bergen-Belsen but not what he saw as the spell time casts on people and societies desperate to believe in its healing powers—for so long I was persuaded by Améry's words.

'Time,' says Frances, 'if anyone asks me, I tell them. It's the only thing.'

The part of her that is turned towards Katie and that will now be permanently shaped that way, that's not most of Frances anymore. It's not like she grew new skin, it's more like she grew new parts.

• • •

One afternoon years ago Frances is over for a cup of tea. I hear my daughter singing in the bathroom "Gloomy Sunday". As sung by Billie Holiday. A song about suicide. Possibly the most beautiful song on the subject ever. *Dearest, the shadows I live with are numberless.* Of all the songs my daughter sings this one goes furthest into me. I still gasp at certain moments, get taken aback by what the song can do to me, does it every time. At first when I hear my daughter's voice I'm mortified Frances might hear. How utterly careless of us. What kind of family are we? Buffoons. Then I think 'actually' and then I think 'bugger it'. Then I ask my daughter to come to the big room and sing it here. The world is big and most of it is not filled with pain and it has a Katie-shaped hole in it. Frances sits straight-backed on the couch. My daughter, Billie, closes her eyes for her namesake's song. 'It's beautiful, it's terrifying,' Frances says when it's finished.

Something she wrote five years after Katie's death

I remember making bargains with myself. I would live life as a quadriplegic to have her back... I would choose to have my lips stitched and not speak another word… I would never have thought I would think this but I don't wish for her to be back. I can't imagine life with her, before I couldn't imagine one without.

• • •

'Hey, Maria,' Frances texts me, 'I am about to bombard you with pages from Katie's school diary. They've made me sad.'

I sit and read. What is there on these pages? Life and death and time (life being the most banal of the lot) all mixed up together like swabs and scalpels after a surgery.

> Japanese. Dentist appointment.
> We don't live in a perfect place.
> Peace doesn't exist.
> chemistry book
> Not in this world or
> Even within ourselves.
> Kickboxing 6:00.

Further down

> It's so easy to erase pencil or a tape.
> I didn't know it could be so easy to
> Erase a life you weren't even a
> Mistake.
> Methods (tech) 8.30—10.45

THOSE WHO FORGET THE PAST
ARE CONDEMNED TO RE—

NEWSPAPER INTRO. 'The couple who abducted their grandson and hid him in a makeshift dungeon were jailed yesterday.'

They are in their fifties, born in Poland. Judge declares the grandmother, this woman, the LEADER IN THE AFFAIR. She is sentenced to fifteen months' jail and has to serve a minimum five. Her husband gets twelve suspended. In court records the woman is referred to as an artist, and that she is.

The MAKESHIFT DUNGEON is in a way-out Melbourne suburb and is the length of a single bed.

Apart from the bed there's a TV, small table, chair, an ornament or two, no windows. During what the Judge calls a FOUR MONTHS' ORDEAL the GRANDSON who's twelve reads, watches TV, and writes. He is only in the room, which is concealed by a moulded rock wall, when police come to his grandparents' house. Which is to say twelve times at least from the day he disappears from a local primary school on a September afternoon. Police know the missing boy had lived in the house with his father and grandparents from when he was a few months old till his father died and his mother, estranged till then, sued for custody. Sued for custody and won. Police turn the place upside down. One time they bring a seismic sensor and fibre-optic cameras, another time they start drilling while the many dogs of the house bark loud and long.

In charge the Detective Senior Constable, a determined man, gives the story to a female Crime Reporter, the only one at her newspaper. She describes him as someone 'who lives and breathes his cases'. He has done all he can and now police need the story to break in the media. It's pre-internet times, newspapers are in rude health still and they get things done. The story is frontpage material. Alleged kidnapping of a minor with possible international twist—suggestions fly that the father's side of the family may fatten the boy up, change his hair colour, and get him out of the country. The detective and the reporter have worked together before. 'He trusted me with reporting the cases,' she says. 'Trusted me not to go overdramatic.' Crime Reporter likes it that the Detective Senior Constable gets particularly worked up over cases involving children. Right now he wants to reunite the missing boy with his mother. The newspaper coverage does the trick. Sometime in January an employee at a car rental joint in another city calls 000 with a tip-off.

When the woman is arrested her grandson is by her side and the name she gives to police is that of her own mother. The ID she shows them belongs to her mother too. In the woman's paintings her mother appears as an aristocrat (the palette is pastel, almost see-through) clad in elegant clothing from another era, garments too big for her small, strong body. At different times and to different people the woman will describe her mother as 'the bravest person I know'. To me she will say, 'My mum had that strength. All through her life. When other people were unable to bear that kind of load, she could.

Watching her made me stronger still. I became a master of strength.'

Crime Reporter meets the boy's mother while the boy is still missing. The mother looks distraught. It's Christmas time just about and not having her son for Christmas is, she says, hard. 'Some mothers,' the Crime Reporter tells me, 'have repulsed me over the years. Not this one.' The mother asks the reporter not to publish her fiance's name. Unusual request—most people are fine with having their names in print—the reporter doesn't think too much about it. 'If I'd had the surname,' she says now, 'I would have done some investigations. But I didn't know who he was.'

Only one journalist, in another paper, with the matter in court already, publishes the man's surname and a single sentence connecting the man to the boy's decision to run away and seek his grandparents' protection. The man's name is not mentioned again.

After that the boy is with his mother, not just the mother, with his brother and half-sister too, all the siblings living together, the half-sister's a few years older, the brother a few years younger, and the mother's 'fiance', who is the half-sister's father, is also in the house with them after more than a decade inside Pentridge's A Division. The mother thanks the media and the police for bringing her son home. Tears etc. The boy will need a lot of intensive counselling, the mother says. Journalists—not the Crime Reporter, she's finished up on this story, but the ones at her newspaper who cover families coming together or falling apart—write of the boy speeding on a bike up and down neighbourhood streets. The bike, full speed, is the sign that all is as it should be. Child, mother, brother, sister, stepfather, house, bike.

The woman is charged with child-stealing her grandson and spends two months on remand in Deer Park Women's Correctional Centre. Detective Senior Constable, who likes children to be safe, opposes her bail application though not her husband's. He gets released after ten days. He, says the Detective Senior Constable, was happy how things were with the boy's mother keeping custody and the grandparents getting fortnightly visits; it's the grandmother who has BRAINWASHED the grandson. 'Everything that has gone wrong,' the detective is quoted saying, 'was directly because of the grandmother.' The court hears of two years of letters written by the boy and grandmother to the Department of Human Services requesting the boy be returned to his grandparents' care. The letters, dismissed by the DHS and the Family Court, are according to the detective evidence of the grandmother's custody fixation. This brainwashing of the lost-now-found boy seems to be the answer to a whole lot of questions—why'd he walk out by himself from school? What made him write those letters? Why ask his grandparents for help?

A visitor, the Chaplain, goes to see the woman at Deer Park and notes that the woman spends most of her time painting. 'Nobody likes being locked up,' the Chaplain tells me, 'it's a real shock. Still, she was the most privileged prisoner I'd met. They gave her canvases, they gave her paints, they gave her a room.' The woman paints a series of works that get exhibited at Old Melbourne Gaol when bail finally comes through. Her paintings, says the Chaplain—only Jewish chaplain in Victoria—are 'expansive, and alternative, and abstract, and beautiful. And really colourful. And very sensual.' The woman has a gift for lifting what's harrowing towards vitality writes the critic who writes the exhibition catalogue essay. Colour is the other gift. It is a force.

'In jail,' the woman says to me years later, 'I was all eyes and ears. I was afraid I would run out of time. Why should you want to get out of a place with so much material? It's crazy to say this. I shouldn't be saying it. But this is what I feel.'

Nine months after bail comes sentencing. The woman and her husband plead guilty—on the advice of an experienced Criminal Barrister they hire. The reasons for their actions will come out in court—says the Criminal Barrister.

Only it doesn't happen that way. The promised surge of attention away from the grandparents towards the grandson's welfare never materialises.

'If I were a lawyer,' the woman says, 'and maybe I am wrong because I am only a painter, I would probably shout the reasons to the court.'

Criminal Barrister has since passed away from cancer so *she* can't explain why she couldn't stop things going so wrong.

Court Psychologist asked to assess the woman tells the court of the woman's grief flowing from the sudden death of her only child, the boy's father. Killed in a motorcycle accident two and a half years earlier but the grief is still acute. Court Psychologist says the woman is not psychotic, obsessive, schizophrenic or suicidal. Court Psychologist has been doing this court thing forever: Magistrate's, County, Supreme, Family, Children's. He spends two hours with the woman. 'I wasn't myself,' the woman tells me. 'If you slap a dog, a dog is not himself.' The grief the Court Psychologist seems to fasten on to is there, that's a given, it'll always be there, but meanwhile the woman's belief that her grandson is in danger in his mother's house is mentioned only in passing.

No one who is aware, however dimly, of a man with an armed robbery and an aggravated burglary to his name, other priors too, plus a history of drug dealing inside and outside, seems to have any interest in following up on what the woman is saying about him. More than a decade inside Pentridge and now he's inside a house with three young kids and it's like the man is invisible, a ghost, and the woman about to head back to jail cannot make anyone see him. Instead everyone sees her: weird, unhinged, smothering, duplicitous, foreign. The media is for the most part peddling dungeons and airless basements, brainwashing and outrageous abductions, with, by way of an overarching framework, angry climaxes to festering hostilities. It's a good story, a great story, and they got it from the police, horse's mouth, besides there is never enough time to dig and why would you when everything fits so nicely together as is? 'We write and publish one-tenth of what's out there,' the Crime Reporter says to me. 'One time I had seventeen minutes to write a frontpage story.'

Crime Reporter does not think the woman is a criminal. What she did was an 'extreme reaction to what a lot of families go through'. Extreme? The woman would say hers was the only possible reaction to the phone call her grandson made after walking out of schoolgrounds—I am not going back to that house no matter what, he'd said. 'I used to be such a law-abiding citizen before this,' the woman says to me. 'Would never break a single traffic rule.' Crime Reporter will give up the crime beat once she has her own kids: too dangerous this work if you have a family. Six years later the Judge will retire, become a Reserve Judge. The woman believes he was made to retire and that her case had a lot to do with it.

The sentencing:

Judge acknowledges the grandparents' clean record and concern for the boy's safety. States he has no choice but to jail them. The offence is too severe, one count of taking away a child under sixteen, one count of false testimony, BAREFACED LIES rules the Judge, who describes what the grandparents did as outrageous, manipulative, extensive, elaborate, sophisticated. He calls it a SCHEME. The boy is victim of an UNFORTUNATE TUG OF WAR leaving him confused and troubled. Judge has no comment on whether the grandparents' fears for the child's wellbeing are justified. He talks rousingly about the boy's mother's suffering, her not knowing for months where her son was, her being scared out of her mind. He doesn't mention—does he not know?—that the mother did not see her son for close to ten years. He doesn't mention—this he certainly doesn't know—that the man back from Pentridge now walks around the house with a knife. One day the Judge's daughter will be walking around with a knife too, stopping women with children, pregnant bellies, old faces and making them give her whatever they have in their wallets to feed her heroin habit. It's far away, this stuff, unimaginable to the Judge. Right now in this courtroom he's on a roll.

The woman about to be jailed has several theories on why the Judge is so burned up by her case, one theory being he is scandalised at the suggestion, which in his head has become a fact, that she is trying to replace her dead son with the grandson. The court hears from the mother that the woman, this grandmother, offered to adopt the boy. This is true. Mention is made of the woman's own son's ashes. How they're on her mantelpiece. 'I never wanted to replace my son, my son is not replaceable,' the woman says to me. Whatever else is going on for the Judge, he is clearly reacting to how the woman in front of him loves her twelve-year-old grandson. In the Judge's head this love, mixed up with loss, has crossed lines not to be crossed. It has become dangerous, immoral.

The stone:

The woman, grandmother, artist, mastermind, whatever you want to call her, says nothing, just sits emotionlessly as the Judge speaks. Her silence is noted by journalists present. One describes her as stone-faced. Another, given to psychological insights, mentions her history as a child Holocaust survivor from Warsaw who stayed alive by hiding. She is still hiding, he writes, and makes it his last sentence. It is not apparent to any-one in that courtroom, least of all the Judge, that the woman's silence is an expression of disgust not shock. 'In media reports,' she will say to me years later, 'you might have noticed them talking about me not saying anything, not showing any emo-tions. If they had asked me why I said nothing—nobody asked me, but if they did—I would have said *I had nobody to talk to*. And when people say to me why didn't you bring this or that up I say *there was no one to bring it up to*. When I was in the court-room, what can I tell you… I felt above it. Above it all. I talked to myself. I looked at the judge and thought you little piglet. I had nothing to say.'

The woman was born in Warsaw in April 1943. Nothing Jewish was being born in Warsaw at this time. The ghetto was burning. Everyone like her was dead or dying. Her grandparents, her brother four years older, her father: killed. But there she was hiding with her mother in a deep pit where potatoes get stored for winter so they won't be ruined by frost. The pit was covered with straw and sand. A Polish woman, a doctor, a Catholic, who was hiding them, dropped supplies down the hole and picked up the waste. The mother's body heat kept the baby from freezing. In the pit the mother had no moment of peace, convinced they could be discovered, killed anytime. That was the first year of the woman's life. Then Auschwitz.

Inside the Australian jail the woman does not put herself down as Jewish. Jewish in a place of no freedom is the last thing she wants to be. In twenty-four years as a chaplain the Chaplain has seen no anti-Semitism in jail, it's pretty multicultural in there, but the woman is not to know that. She makes contact with the Chaplain through another Jewish prisoner who she sees reading Tehillim, the book of psalms, in Hebrew. The woman and the Chaplain talk for a long time about religion, her family, justice. A jail is a jail though, not a spiritual retreat, prisoners are chucked together. 'You can be a murderer or you could have not paid,' the Chaplain says, 'your parking fines.' Or something drug-related: that accounts for half the women or more. While the woman serves out her sentence another woman, at forty-three, dies from natural causes. Another is found hanging. Some women in jail, particularly newbies, get so scared their legs shake uncontrollably and the Chaplain has to hold their legs down. Not the woman—she seems OK. She is surrounded by other people's suffering and wants to observe, absorb. What do humans do with their pain? What if the pain becomes intolerable? When is there no choice? Where can you go inside yourself from behind the wires?

One of her paintings is called *Poetry of the Jail*. Enclosed by barbed wire ten naked ghostly figures, sexless, indistinguishable from each other, huddle together, imagining—remembering—freedom. Freedom is having red hair that takes up half the sky. Freedom is your breasts glowing like full moons, glistening like melons washed by monsoon rain. In the exhibition catalogue Marc Chagall is cited and not only for colour reasons. ('When Matisse dies,' Picasso said once, 'Chagall will be the only painter left who understands what colour is.') It's also because of the persistence of human figures in the woman's work, no matter the symbolism and her wild playing with colour and form. 'Drop me into an abyss,' she says, 'and I find human expressions and experiences to paint.'

Colours of her prison work: pinkish reds, eyeshadowy blues and purples (think teenage girls, pre-sophisticates), lemon yellows, enshrouding whites.

'I remember thinking about her going to prison,' the Chaplain says, 'for hiding her grandson while her daughter-in-law and people around her were thugs and drug dealers. She'd lost her son. I understood her so clearly, why she did it. The whole situation was insane. I cannot get my head around it.'

Chaplain comes to the woman's house. Chaplain's kids are little. They bring a kosher picnic, and plastic plates, and they befriend the woman's mother and husband—'a beautiful, gentle soul'. The woman's mother's lungs were destroyed in the hiding. She can breathe better in this house far away from traffic, surrounded by trees. The house, thinks the Chaplain, is like something in a movie. 'With a cellar, an attic, surrounded by forest, and no heating.' The driveway is so steeply angled they are frightened to drive their old eight-seater van up to the entrance. They park at the bottom and walk. Chaplain asks to see the room where the boy was hidden. She's surprised: looks like a boy's room. 'It had a door that looked like part of the wall. A bit like where people were hidden during the war. Otherwise,' she says, 'it was a lovely room with wooden walls.' A psychologist who researches hidden child survivors of the Holocaust sees the room when she comes to interview the woman for her dissertation. For her the parallels are uncanny and she writes: 'To step into her home in a remote part of Melbourne where she lived with her husband and elderly mother was to experience a stepping back in time to Poland under the Nazi regime. There was nothing ostensibly in the environment which provoked this image, yet the atmosphere was unquestionably so.'

Psychologist was thrown too by the driveway's steepness. Oh boy. Did it ever require some kamikaze driving.

The grandparents are forbidden from seeing their grandson for nine years until he is twenty-one and can make his own choices. They have no money or avenues left to fight the court's order. The woman tries to 'develop rage for' the boy's mother but that's easier said than done. She was the one to search for the mother in the first place while the boy's father was still alive. To deprive a child of a living mother is a travesty—that's what she believed and why she went looking. A child's mother may be absent, troubled, have a drug problem, but still you have to try. The woman's own mother is her biggest hero. The bond they have—had it from day one—is sacred. 'My mother survived bravely,' she says. 'My father was an exceptionally brave man who simply couldn't survive. My mother lived till ninety-eight and could have lived another ten. She had cancer and they refused to do chemo because of her age, which I cannot forgive them for.'

She cannot hate the boy's mother: 'My son said she had rocks in her head. That man could have easily killed her. One more punch another time and she could have been dead. She lost her teeth. Her children had to clean up pools of blood after their mother was beaten to a pulp.' This mother was a victim too but she, no, didn't, couldn't, protect her boys (from what the woman understands the man spared his daughter, left her alone, it's impossible to know for sure). The mother has 'sunk into trouble', the woman says. It is possible to *sink into trouble* you know.

If only the woman could have known the man was out of jail when she went looking for the boy's mother. Yes, she did offer to adopt, at her own son's funeral actually. No-brainer it seemed like: the boy had always been with them and this way he'd be safe, looked after, raised with knowledge of their history and customs, and the house could go to him when they were dead. The 'tug of war' only started a certain while after the motorcycle accident. One factor—you can speculate about others—was the traffic accident compensation, a considerable amount, to be paid out to each child of the parent killed.

Rage she cannot feel for the boy's mother she feels for the institutions supposed to keep all children safe. She feels it for Australia: 'I came to this country thinking it was a civilised society. How wrong I was. It's a wild, wild West. A modern country filled with barbarians. How else could such a terrible injustice occur, and my two grandsons be put in mortal danger by the lawmakers of this country?' The other grandson always lived with the mother; she has no history with him, no deep connection. Only love and a sense of intolerable injustice.

Attached to a feature article in a long since defunct independent magazine are photographs of the woman in the forest near her house. She is looking up at sky, to the ground, into the distance, down the camera. In yet another photograph she stands next to her husband, he's in a suit, her in a white blouse, she is cradling a dog. The woman's mother, still alive, is sitting in front holding a photograph of the boy in a bow tie. Behind the three of them are the woman's works. Startling, large, vortex-like.

'What happened to me is not normal, is it?'

When we first make contact her voice on the phone takes me by surprise. Young, girlish, with a vibrancy in it I didn't expect, a femininity. A few minutes into our conversation someone is at the door, she's apologising ('I'm terribly sorry, Maria') and going to see who is there, while dogs bark, and on the dogs go for ten minutes. I imagine police. Ripping into the house. We live in the same city but she feels far away. I tell her I know she is worried about her grandsons, I promise to do no harm, whatever I write will be scrubbed clean of identifying details. 'Don't worry about me, Maria, I am a survivor in my life, I have enough strength for this,' she says. 'It's a terribly powerful thing to be a survivor. I am a little person structurally but I do possess a tremendous spirit. I had to deal with all sorts of experiences. For other people—too much. For me—no.' The grandson, an adult now, is back in that house police once strived to save him from. I won't speak to him. He is not ready, she says. 'He is yet to learn how to be a survivor.'

The woman tells me, Warsaw was all rubble after the war.

Things were exploding all the time. Walking around was really dangerous. We were walking in this city of rubble, she says, and I had a little bag of treasures, broken glass and somesuch. And I found this doll. My mother was terrified because the doll was so ugly but I absolutely loved it. I clutched it in my arms. I mean, what were the chances of me, a Jewish child, being alive after the war, being alive in Warsaw, and finding this doll?

In the woman's painting of that postwar moment the child is wearing a bonnet and her hair is in careful curls, as if she came from a world where children were dainty things, dressed-up cherubs. Not gassed, killed point-blank, thrown against walls, starved, handed over for medical experiments. The doll's face is below her Adam's apple. She is holding it tight. The ugly, dirty, flaccid cloth doll.

We arrange to meet. Crossed wires, me at the wrong place, right time, she doesn't own a mobile phone and I am about to go, thinking que sera sera, when a fire at a nearby station— second time it happened to me in twenty-five years in Australia—halts all trains. A taxi home would be two hundred bucks. I get on a bus to make my way to a different station, alternative train line, two stops in my phone rings. We are meant to meet after all. She is tiny.

I knew someone from the genocidal wars of Bosnia who refused, for the longest time, to get herself a mobile phone. I thought a phone in your pocket is another layer of protection. For her it was the opposite. Maybe after certain kinds of experiences it is simply not possible to ever feel safe again and the best you can hope for is to feel inaccessible. Hidden. The woman has a coffee in a takeaway cup in a cafe near the place where we finally meet. My five-fruit juice has an orange lid.

She says her coffee is so bad it's good. I say my juice is as you would expect. We can talk but no recording. 'They said I did something outrageous. What they did was a million times more outrageous. If there was a medal for outrageous they would get the medal.' They: Judge, Detective Senior Constable, media, Department of Human Services, Family Court, County Court, Australian public, the country of Australia.

She thinks someone somewhere down the line got bought, I am less sure. What she wants to know is who was paying who, who intimidating who. I am thinking a miscarriage of justice in the world of abused and neglected children is as common as primary school nits. Part of the problem, as criminologist Kerry Carrington writes, is 'the administrative apparatus surrounding the children's courts [does] not distinguish between neglected children or delinquent children'. Children get taken away when they shouldn't, abused in foster families or institutions, left in danger with their own families, forced to be someone else's responsibility, pushed up and down the chain like containers of mercury. Plus most kids would choose sticking with their family over safety so it's fraught on all sides. Surely the wilful blindness around the boy's predicament was partly structural, bureaucratic, the system's stretched and faltering, no, let me put it differently—the system is fucking plenty of children up; it's kind of impersonal.

I ask a handful of people who know some of what happened how could it end up like this? For four months with redhot zeal a boy is searched for only to be fed to wolves once found. People reply (a) the justice system is broken and makes a heap of mistakes, (b) the media just wants a good story, (c) the judge was probably an old Australian fuddy-duddy and the fuddy-duddies don't like 'em foreigners and especially 'em foreigners not playing along with our system, (d) the cop looking for the boy must have felt humiliated, and (e) there is something we don't know. I'd like to ask the detective (unlikely he'd give me much) but can't. I swore to do nothing to make the boy or family unsafe. The woman counts the Detective Senior Constable as an enemy for life.

A retired senior journalist tells me cops would have been pissed off with the woman—she made them look like fools, lied to them repeatedly, broke the law. More than pissed off enough for them to turn on her. As for the Judge, journalists knew he had a troubled domestic life and shared an unspoken agreement to not mention it, both out of compassion and so as not to piss him off.

'He is not corrupt,' the journalist says, 'there is nothing on him.'

There is an (f) here too that no one mentions: *her*. In this country, grandmothers—go ahead, ask around—don't play cat and mouse with police, don't have rooms in their houses undetectable by special fibre-optic cameras, don't provide someone else's ID when apprehended, don't mis-steer court registrars when quizzed about grandkids' whereabouts (I am referring here to sworn testimony by the woman and her husband during the first month of the boy's 'disappearance' that they had no idea where he'd got to).

Her foreignness. But no one cares. Half the population here has a parent born elsewhere, so say the parent-born-elsewhere stats I've been inserting every time I give one of my 'multicultural' talks. Yet certain foreignnesses are not dissolved in the balmy Australian air. They remain solid, determining of what happens to people so marked when they brush against the hard surfaces of banks, courts, police stations, universities, workplaces or the softer (more porous?) surfaces of shops, trains, city streets. In no nation on this planet is this not the everyday usual. Still you have to ask—why what she did felt so foreign here, like such anathema? Children taken away from their families, and families, driven berserk by fear, grandmothers included, trying to hide their kids from authorities (in the bush, under the house, with other families, skin covered with mud)—how foreign is this story? How outside the range of easily conjurable? Surely it is one of the key stories of this WILD, WILD WEST country too.

> Grandmothers feel like they have responsibilities and obligations to their grandchildren and that responsibility is being ripped away from us. Grandmothers put their hands up, they say we're here. And generally they had shared care of these children. They were primary carers of these children and they are bypassed... These are women who are educated women, they've got degrees, they've got no criminal history, they've got no drug or alcohol issues and these people are overlooked. They are going to court for months... Then the Department and the Magistrate decides no and that's how it goes.

So goes an interview on Radio National with a representative of Grandmothers Against Removals, a network of grandmothers fighting the mass removal of indigenous children from their families by, in their words, 'child *protection* services, police, and juvenile prisons'. It's February 2015.

Psychologist's parents were kids, Jewish, in World War II, both surviving in hiding. This—hidden Jewish children—is her lifelong subject. She cannot fail to recognise, when she interviews the woman for her dissertation, how the woman describes her year in the potato pit almost 'as if her mother's memories were her own'. And, for the woman, when her mother used to talk about what happened she'd feel like her mother's experiences were her experiences. After the war the mother showed her places: where she was born, where her father and brother were killed, where the mother fainted and the lady Catholic doctor saw her and subsequently hid them. The potato pit was no longer there but the rest she could see. In every bit of their conversation the Psychologist, who has spent much of her adult life immersed in child survivors' stories, cannot escape a feeling, 'an eerie sense of history repeating'.

'No, no, I wasn't hiding him,' the woman said to the Psychologist.

But then, sometime later, 'for me the Holocaust continues in a miniature form'.

'She was so young when she was hidden,' the Psychologist tells me, 'that language wasn't there. When it is pre-verbal, and when experiences and emotions do not have language attached to them, they go inside our body and we do not have the same awareness of them.'

Here is a way to make pieces fit—the woman's childhood and the makeshift dungeon, the pit and the Deer Park Women's Correctional Centre, half a century and a different continent later. A particular way of thinking about trauma hands it to us. First look away from what happened to the boy. Focus on the woman: like the Judge, the Court Psychologist, the Detective Senior Constable did. Accept that the woman continues to be traumatised (this cannot but be true) by what happened to her during the war, and has been acting out. Faced with danger, she digs a potato pit for her grandson in the middle of suburban Australia. She treats police like an SS squad. Judge is, I don't know, some high-up Nazi. Behind him the machinery of the complicit State is churning over like a song. The boy's mother is like one of those Poles who denounced their Jewish neighbours out of fear and greed, not sadism, not adherence to some ideology. In other words the woman's behaviour and judgment are impaired by trauma. ('Impaired' too harsh? Consider 'profoundly affected'.) Maybe if the Court Psychologist talked in court about the war, not her grief, the Judge would have been not so resolute in his condemnation.

Mention the war.

Don't.

'The reason I speak with such disgust about the so-called justice system here,' the woman says to me, 'is not because I am some poor victimised traumatised child survivor and this is just another layer. No, this has nothing to do with my old trauma. What I am telling you is that something absolutely terrible, tragic happened in Australia and the justice system let it happen, made it happen.'

Can you see what she is saying?—do not use the horrors of my childhood to cancel out what happened to my grandson, do not use my trauma to cover up the vast compounded injustice that smashed my family. Here, in this country. Don't use my tragedy to mask your moral failure. When the woman says, as she does repeatedly, that the war is not over for her, you can take it that she is trapped in the past inside that old war she was not supposed to survive, or you may contemplate that WAR is a word for her grandson being sent back to his torturer while she is deposited in jail. In the name of justice, huzzah! War is the two of them waiting nearly a decade to see each other again.

Jail is the last thing it's about for her.

She says, they killed my little brother by smashing his head on the pavement. They cannot hurt me anymore because I am already so hurt. 'What,' she says, 'could they do to me, how long could they jail me for? Hundred years?' I lost my whole family apart from my mother in the Holocaust, she says.

It is about the boy.

She pulls out a photograph. 'Look at his eyes. He came back to us at twenty-one. Already an alcoholic. He went through such things. Didn't tell me most things. He cannot talk about them. If he even mentions anything, he is not himself, he cannot bear mentioning it.'

If it is in any sense about her, it is about her not honouring a promise to her son to protect his child and keep together what is left of the family.

After what her mother did to protect her.

In Australia everything is turned on its head—who's in jail and who's not, what counts as a crime, the good guys get pounded, the bad guys are whipped with feather dusters. My husband, she says, he's in his seventies. Works twelve-hour shifts, pays taxes, so that the man who abused her grandson can get 'a nice relaxing time in jail, good meals'. And so he 'can watch TV with all the movies in which they kill each other and cut each other and eat each other and he can have a lovely rest, get himself healthy and well, and get ready to come out and start terrorising my grandsons'.

'Do you think I am an outlaw, Maria?'

Loïc Wacquant called prisons 'outlaw institutions'. He said they violate, 'necessarily and routinely', the very societal laws they are presumed to uphold and enforce. It's probably Sociology 101 or Criminology 102 but to me it's news. 'Actually,' says the woman, 'prison was more civilised than the whole system outside'—she means more civilised than the justice system—'you know, when I was giving false testimony one time when they still hadn't found him I looked at this judge's eyes and he stared at me for two minutes at least and I stared at him for two minutes because what I wanted to tell him and couldn't was that no court in the world and no judge in the world had the right to put this little boy in such a terrible unsafe situation.' It was a different judge she was staring at that time. Not the Judge who jailed her and put the boy back in the mother's house—'Because I knew about another so-called civilised people somewhere else who did a lot of barbaric things,' she says, 'I was not surprised.'

To be born in the worst time imaginable, what does that leave you with? And to then survive? The doctor hiding them had to go away for a few days and the woman's mother decided the potato pit was no longer safe so they climbed up. They were caught and sent to Auschwitz but by then the war was nearly ending, the baby was a toddler, and even though people were still being gassed the mother and the daughter sneaked out. They found the lady doctor, lived with her, this time above ground. Years passed. The woman married one of the doctor's sons (the doctor had twins). In time the woman, her husband, their young son and the woman's mother left Poland. Too much blood was spilt in Poland, too much hatred could not be erased and the anti-Semitism was unrelenting. The in-laws were deeply anti-Semitic too: the lady doctor, the saintly rescuer, turned out to be as bad as her husband who openly and feverishly hated Jews. (That's a little side-parable for those who think wars are over when they appear to be over. Or that people pick their sides and stay on them. Or that we become our parents. The lady doctor's son who married the woman did not become his mum or dad.) First the four of them went to Israel then they ended up in Australia, Australia being an escape from Poland, in-laws, anti-Semitism, war.

There are people in Australia and of Australia who help the woman. A politician, a future State Liberal Minister—the woman considered the Politician a friend and believes he looked after her while she was in jail. He was the one who forced the Judge to resign too, that's what she thinks. In his memoirs the Politician thanks his parents for not having a single argument in front of him, for making sure their children 'did not wit-ness the less attractive expressions of their emotions'. He is no longer alive. She thinks of him a lot. Another good one is the Prison Director. He too goes on to become a boss man presid-ing over one correctional services conglomerate or another. A cousin of the man who got out of Pentridge's A Division was in the same jail as the woman and, the way it looked to people smart to that world, her life was in danger. So the Prison Direc-tor, says the woman, ordered guards to follow her. Good people are everywhere, she's seen and met plenty.

It's the system failure, the culture failure. The blindness. It is like the twentieth century didn't quite happen here, not in the same way anyway, a century that, in its closing decades at the very least, made whole societies fearful of barbarity, violence, fanaticism within and without, because people now knew how close these things were to the surface, what little it took to unleash them, and how once they were out there they destroyed wholesale 'the very structures of civilised life' as Tony Judt wrote—'regulations, laws, teachers, policemen, judges'—scooping up informal structures of reciprocity and trust along the way. Not that countries in Europe or Asia or Africa that remember what wars do are immune or enlightened—Yugoslavia!—and not that intergenerationally things are not lost—Cambodia!—and not that remembering wars can ever be free from the dirty politics of the present—Russia!—and not that remembering is always a self-evident good, but still.

The woman who talks of WWII, brings it up again and again, her whole being insisting it is necessary to put it at the centre of the table seventy years after its end, especially in *this* country, which she says is *filled with barbarians*, could she be on to something? The remembering she does, which the world around her sees as her trauma taking over, her soul ulcer screaming out, could it be that this remembering is what this country needs? Not the pomp of it, brass bands and hands over heart, but the horror of it that lives under the skin of a culture and makes the culture worry sick about where it's going and what it may miss.

When Tony Judt wrote that in the 21st century the United States was exceptional in the way it had forgotten 'the meaning of war'—surely the most important historical lesson of the century before it—he was forgetting Australia where the forgetting of war is double. The first thing forgotten is the war fought in this country, which *has not had a war fought on its soil*: a hundred and forty years' worth of ubiquitous and continuous frontier conflict glimmering for so long in the space between remembering and forgetting, recalled in stops and starts now, still not recognised publicly as a WAR. The other forgetting is more the kind Judt was talking about, things witnessed on other shores, what wars do to people and to everything they love and build.

The woman doesn't wish any suffering on this country and its people, doesn't begrudge it being spared. In Australia people did not have to learn that 'a human being becomes an animal in three weeks—with the hard work, cold, hunger and beatings' (Varlam Shalamov, writer, Gulag survivor). Of course it is a blessing not to have this twentieth-century lesson home delivered. Of course the only adequate response to this bless-ing is infinite gratitude. But it can't be a cover for ignorance. Or indifference. Being spared means you have to work twice as hard at remembering. Only when does that ever happen? Two words: 'human nature'. She knows.

Two decades later the woman and her husband will do the paperwork, leave the house to the young man and his younger brother, and move out of Melbourne. No one will tap them on the shoulder and say, 'Forgive us for we got you so wrong. You were not criminals after all but righteous people. You were not criminals but loyal, loving grandparents. You acted the only way you could. You acted the way civilised people must act.' No one will apologise to the young man either for not letting him save himself (he did what he could and where did it get him?). No one, not even god.

• • •

(g)

'I now know what I didn't know when we last spoke,' the woman says. 'Judge got bribed.

'Detective Senior Constable was involved in cover-ups and crime.

'My son was killed.

'A trap was set for me.

'They knew I would do anything for my grandson.'

The woman is wearing a white blouse and grey pants. I've only ever seen her in white tops. Her husband is mowing the lawn. He'll go slowly, take his breaks, but he'll get it done. Shall we have a cup of tea while we talk? No. Yes. No. Too much to say.

Her eyes.

'I can read between the lines,' the woman says. 'I know who my grandson would choose even though he knows I am his best friend.'

Even when filled with tears, they are scooping the world from inside out, peering into the far-out corners of it. Even when they are crying, they are smiling at the bottomlessness of human endurance.

Outside of Melbourne the woman and her husband have two rooms and a little verandah. The yard, and the care for it, is shared between three families. She is painting and feels maybe it's a whole new period she's entering. 'Painting is about the illusion of depth, you do it through perspective. About bringing people into it. But what I am working on is bringing the painting out.'

The woman always thought what happened to her family in Australia was criminal—not only isn't-it-outrageous criminal, not yet-another-failure-of-criminal-justice-system criminal, but criminal-criminal—and now she's sure beyond doubt. Judge. Detective Senior Constable. Bought. Bloodied. *All that for a house.* Worth millions now, true, even so. Greed: who could have foretold that out of seven sins (still seven?) it'd be the one to do her family in? Such a toothless little badness compared to what else is out there. Australia… Australia…

I want to say to her I can't believe she'll have to live with never knowing for certain what happened. So much of her new information cannot be verified without a full-scale cold case investigation that'll potentially implicate police and judiciary and the likelihood of that ever kickstarting? Negligible. I say nothing. The woman is convinced the people who found her recently and confirmed her son's murder and her own entrapment are to be trusted. Her gut knew it all along and her heart is now moving away from the grandson—that same love for him inside her, but no more saving him. Someone else will need to keep him safe from the house. From the temptation of robbing her. Or maybe he won't be saved. The *Drowned and the Saved* as Primo Levi put it back when. 'The harsher the oppression, the more widespread among the oppressed is the willingness, with all its infinite nuances and motivations, to collaborate…

'The room for choices (especially moral choices) was reduced to zero.'

Her grandson will discover, doesn't realise it yet, that the house where he and his brother are living is actually not hers so cannot be made his. Theirs. And then it'll be the rest of his life. And he'll hate it and what he'll make of it will be his life's work. She and her husband did their bit. She wants to grow old and paint. She'll never be safe in Australia but can't go anywhere either. She doesn't even like travelling outside Australia. Her son is buried here. Her mother.

She has been re-reading the Torah and the Talmud. Her son was religious ('you didn't know? oh yes, very') and she is trying to get as close as she can to the way he'd be looking at things. Reading Torah means thinking a lot about Eve. Isn't Eve head and shoulders above Adam? A cosmic being. Do you agree, Maria?

Modern Mona Lisa is the name of one of the recent works. She'll show it to me next time. She may have done something there, had a breakthrough. 'I said to Leonardo: *you couldn't do this but I can.*'

We hug like two people on a train platform—strangers who love each other with the love that belongs not to them but to the world around them that has gone off its axis.

His eyes.

His eyes when my car backs out of the driveway.

HISTORY REPEATS ITSELF

THIS MORNING, that morning rather, two men in my carriage lift their heads—two men in their fifties in silky understated ties—then there is a little snap, like a red light camera going off, and even before the next stop gets announced they're leaning into each other laughing how long has it been? Must be forty years give or take. What's been happening? They run through their classmates: two cancers (one mid-chemo, one cannot hack chemo), a property development fraud, one guy (just the other side of a protracted settlement) with too many ex-wives (stupid bastard, he and them deserve each other). A pause. Please don't tell me it's all there is. Fraud, cancer, bad marriage picks, being caught, extricating yourself, chance encounters on city loop trains; can you remember the last time life felt long or kind, or like it was yours and mine?

My phone vibrates: one time only for texts. 'Make sure you don't have scissors, nail files, anything sharp.' It's Vanda. Thank you Vanda.

Shhh.

In front of me is time. Time is not a river. It is two strangers on a train whose briefcases touch as they hold each other. Two men who'll never ride the same train again.

I don't remember getting off or walking. Somehow I

reached the courthouse doors on William Street where my bag was screened, nothing sharp in it, and the structure that looked dull and huge on the outside, a building without qualities, was alive and brown inside with wrappers pulled off chocolate bars, doors slamming, others opening, kids in school uniforms who were not, as I'd guessed, witnesses to inexplicable suburban crimes but legal studies students bored on a field trip. Several of the magistrates looked like Karl Heinrich Marx. In a lift I stood next to a lawyer with the face of someone who sometimes forgets he has not, yet, seen it all. I looked at him. He looked at the crease in his hardworking pants.

What is the Court 8 clerk wearing today? Orange jacket, there you go, bold choice for the setting. And what is Court 8's loudest sound right now? My fineliner pen making notes about courtroom silence. Big silence in a roomful of busy-looking people is jarring. Then the magistrate appears—once he's seated, that silence is gone—and to a man on the stand whose second drink-driving offence is the day's first matter he says, 'I cannot take your past away,' and it is like some subterranean conversation underneath the one everybody can hear is flowing about how to be alive is to be caught in one web or another. 'I know your first offence was twenty years ago but your past doesn't disappear. If police stop you, they'll test you.' The magistrate means it's your last chance, your cufflinks can't save you, the taxes you pay won't save you. He also means: nothing is more human than the experience of feeling trapped. And everything's a trap, your past, family, genes, addictions, loneliness, that feeling that pretty much everyone else is galloping gaily ahead while you are crawling backwards like a lobster or lopsided baby.

All morning I wait for something but nothing much happens. After the man on drink-driving offence #2 comes a retail manager from Elwood who's drinking because her IVF is failing. Next is a well-dressed Somali man charged with not wearing a seatbelt and accompanied by a well-dressed Somali interpreter. After that it's a Turkish taxi driver caught going 105 in an 80 zone. I move courts. Sit in on an aggravated burglary hearing. Go to the room where a meth syndicate (most lawyers I've seen all day) is being sentenced. 'There is no crime of which I do not deem myself capable.' So said Goethe. *Homo sum: humani nil a me alienum puto.* That—'I am human, I consider nothing human alien to me'—is what the Roman playwright Terence said. 'There are no fairytale endings.'

Vanda says that. How come, I ask her.

'Because people are people.'

People wear ugg boots to court. You may find yourself one day staring down at a court floor and seeing ugg boots next to high-heeled, calf-extending leather numbers worn by female lawyers, and this image might lead you to believe that lines have been drawn and you will always be able to tell who is who. Don't believe it. Sometimes it is like that and other times—not at all.

That morning, this morning, I walk back to the station past the cafe where a week ago a deputy chief magistrate, Jelena Popovic, was telling me how it took her years as a magistrate before belatedly understanding that the people appearing in front of her were, in the main, neither offenders nor victims of their own circumstances but rather people at the point of crisis. The crisis was the hopeful thing. 'It started crystallising for me during a late 1990s heroin scourge. It seemed to me we were

doing nothing to help people when we should have been capi-
talising on this point of crisis.' The word, when she said it, had
a nobility, a scale, and seeing myself so struck by it I thought
about how this word, crisis, can recast a human life's broken-
ness. No laughter spilled out of my half-empty afternoon train
home, nobody was falling into an old friend's lap. Each one of
us was alone. With our bags, jackets, leaking umbrellas, wan-
dering eyes, with the big unringing phones we were kneading
in our hands.

I have always dreaded movie sequences in which a human
life—a normal, long life, unshortened by illness or war—gets
condensed into a few emblematic scenes. A child, carefree and
pure, becomes a young adult with shining eyes, then in no time
is a parent of someone whose eyes are soon-to-be shining, and
when next they're beaming out of your screen they are the
same only their hair's greying, eyes woolly, and their frame is
thicker or perhaps slighter, it's as if their form and content are
pulling away from each other, and you know where it is headed,
where else, and despite these characters being fictional and this
life-to-death-in-three-minutes business being just some hillbilly
director's device there is something intolerable about seeing life
with time sucked out of it like the air from an air mattress. A
few occasions, bumping across a movie sequence like that, I'd
put both hands over my chest.

For a long while I could not work out why it hurt. Until I
understood: time. Time is what makes everything OK. How
it flows forward and circles round itself, both; how life, suspended, zero gravity, in time consists of so many things repeating. Getting up, the brushing of hair, toasting of bread, sun
shooting up in the sky, taking keys out of your pocket to open

doors. Seasons. In the benign repetition of daily acts an invisible net is cast, holding people up, protecting them. Because the things being repeated—'non-exchangeable and non-substitutable singularities' so said Deleuze—are never the same. That imperceptible difference, same damn thing, same blessed thing, is what rescues it. So yes those movie sequences hurt. Time as a straight line is a monstrosity. Sometimes though what's being repeated is hope's absence. A child comes into a world that is like a tar pit, a tar pit of prehistoric ferocity, the kind that could suck a Columbian mammoth in. In this world a little creature still sorting its hind legs from its front legs does not stand a chance. Cannot stand. Time is not a river pushing people forward as they lunge at floating branches—inelegantly, so what?—but an oily, seeping substance. Black and sticky.

Most of Vanda's clients come from a tar pit. The term regularly used, 'entrenched disadvantage', is ugly like much of the language to do with people who don't get to do much choosing in their lives, and whose every creep forward—in a good year every couple of creeps—gets followed by a bone-splintering triple tumble backwards. Poverty, abuse, addiction, mental health stuff, they are what's in the tar, the sticky parts.

We met by accident in North Melbourne Town Hall's corridors the spring that I was pregnant with my second child and Vanda was volunteering at a fringe festival. She was checking tickets at the door, helping out with shows. The shows (as you'd expect) were of varying quality. I wondered what she was doing here, this woman whose big polymath mind was straight-away apparent even to me who was sick with a round-the-clock morning sickness and not noticing much. I remember thinking I don't get the whole community volunteering thing. Thinking also that in another time/place this woman could have led armies to battle. I did not know then that she loved theatre, directing, actors—actors especially—and years before had started a theatre company for young people which had a policy of turning away no one at auditions. The result was large, happy casts and full houses. I wasn't aware then that after a disheartening year doing articles at a suburban law firm she needed to feel surrounded by theatre to feel OK. And I was there why? Involved in one of the festival shows if you must know. In a non-performing capacity and due any minute to alight on the discovery of how lucky writers are compared to the men and women of theatre. Writers are not required to be present at their trials.

That first time we talked it occurred to me that with Vanda being a community lawyer the two of us could even be in the same taxation bracket. Not until years later in a St Kilda legal branch foyer, me waiting for Vanda, she running late after a client appointment, did I seconds before she appeared (wearing black and white) write in my notebook, quickly, as if somehow I'd forget it

DECREPIT

SHODDY

FALLING APART

ALARM CODE ON A STICKER

HEATERS EVERYWHERE

COLD

and then deeper inside that building, Vanda's office was like a room from my childhood, windowless, boxy, held together as we'd say 'by an honest word'. Closer to an anti-office. Not long after that in the Magistrate's Court I overheard a young female lawyer say to Vanda, 'I couldn't do what you're doing,' and although it was mostly clear what she meant—couldn't be so near other people's shit and misery, couldn't have the office you have—I tried hard, tried and failed, to figure out if she meant it as a compliment.

The lawyer said what she said after Mike almost fell on her. I was there, saw it, Mike was up before a magistrate on charges of grabbing a fifty dollar note out of the hands of a woman about to pay for her lunch. As Mike, his balance shot, his eyes half closed, teetered in the young female lawyer's vicinity an uncontrolled tiny revulsion burst pink on her cheeks, a similar facial phenomenon, I'm guessing, to the one on the lunching woman's face in that South Melbourne cafe. First Mike had asked the woman for money. 'No.' I too frequently say no and I'd jump as well, as she did, at my bubble being burst even though it's as far away as ever from bursting. While grabbing the note Mike said 'I'll have fifty dollars please' to the woman. Like he was winking and inviting her to share in his pinch of good fortune. Vanda and the police prosecutor both smiled at this point in the prosecutor's account—at Mike's preference for a social intercourse. Bolting away from the woman he got run down by helpful witnesses.

Vanda had represented Mike before and Mike, let's be clear, had taken giant dosages of prescription medication on the mornings of his various other hearings too. On one occasion he was drifting away and no one stirred him so he slept right through. This time Vanda was keeping an eye on things. With clients hanging out, no methadone on them, I've seen her apply for adjournments: them sweating, getting fidgety, feeling sick, not worth it. Pills are a different kettle of fish and Mike did not seem too bad this morning other than, as time passed, he had less and less control over what his body was doing. These meds he'd taken, it turns out, were a bit strong. By the time he got inside the courtroom he was disoriented, talking noticeably overloudly then snapping into sleep. They're precisely things you do not do in court. You whisper unless addressed by a magistrate, in which case you reply softly and with deference, and whatever you do you keep awake, especially when it's your transgression about to be ruled on and this ruling, no matter the ridiculousness of the offence, could return you to jail.

Vanda shushes Mike while arguing for exceptional circum-stances—some months beforehand Mike found his girlfriend dead, from an overdose, in bed—and next breath nearly she's imploring him:

'Mike, don't go to sleep.

'Mike, you must…'

Mike's lips, framed by oozing sores, make the sweet lapping sounds of somebody small, in soft pyjamas, savouring their dreams. He tries waking, swigs from a cup of water Vanda got him but soon his head's nodding, and dropping, while water from the plastic cup's dripping on the court's floor. You don't spill water in court and, if you do, do it fast not in this gradual tipping and dripping way. Nor do you keep your mobile on, volume up, letting it ring out twice while the air in the court-room stiffens until the whole thing feels like a scene from *Duck Soup* and it's two minutes to lunchbreak, which was when Mike virtually fell on the young female lawyer, and the young female lawyer recoiled and looked at Vanda.

Something else farcical: the obviousness of the distance in that room between officialdom and people's lives.

'Sentencing is a construct of the privileged classes,' deputy chief magistrate Popovic says to me. 'I have been doing this job for over twenty years and just worked it out.'

Mike, asleep, noisy, moaning, water funnelling out of his hands, his phone ringing like the immortal shoe phone of Maxwell Smart in the middle of Washington's Symphony Hall, for a moment made the courtroom unspool.

How my head was aching by lunch. Vanda was unflustered. Many people she represents have or had addictions. Most self-medicate. 'My clients,' she says, 'are better at self-medicating than the rest of us, they know which drugs work for them.' Scientific studies are looking into possible positive effects of MDMA on people with PTSDs. Vanda's clients worked that one out years ago. They know what drugs stop bad memories flooding their heads. True, theirs isn't the covert, after-hours self-medication the general populace practises. Vanda's clients don't typically try hard to hide their methods of keeping sane or numb, which is the same thing some of the time, not all of the time. Then when they get picked up for possession, Vanda thinks 'for fuck's sake there are people in this courtroom, lawyers, clerks, who'll go out and take their drug of choice tonight'. Birds do it, bees do it. It's a question of who gets picked up—and you know who. Not that Vanda is all gooey on the subject, too many clients continue overdosing and dying. When one client, Rex, on a specialist assessment list for people with mental health issues and cognitive impairments, was pacing a small interview room before his years-old assault charges hearing, breathing in great gusts, screaming with vehemence—'Police is fucking corrupt! This is not justice! And *I* am supposed to follow the law?'—Vanda preferred him that way, angry, more himself, not numbed out of his skull.

Question of priorities: how much spare energy is there to spend on worrying about accidentally body-slamming an easily spooked and crisp-shirted lady lawyer in Court 7? If you are used to being seen as a public nuisance, why bother tiptoeing in imaginary slippers through the hallowed halls of venerable institutions? Is it not the institutions' problem that they often cannot handle people who don't have the luxury of keeping private business private? Many of Vanda's clients live their lives in public, like Lani who for years resided under trees— at a friend's house, in a park—and who resembled in Vanda's words a 'malignant streetworker fairy on the other side of the faraway tree' which was a change from the nice middle-class life she apparently led before her fairy days. Vanda tells me of a time Lani tried entering the Magistrate's Court with whisky. When Vanda stopped her Lani downed the bottle in one go. Then went in. Another time a security device erupted and Lani was asked to remove her boots (long, long boots they were). 'She takes off her boots and everything apart from the kitchen sink is there—cigarettes, money, phone.'

The pleasure I get in Vanda's Lani stories is the old-as-the-world pleasure of feeling, even secondhand, an anarchic force disrupt orderly proceedings. 'This police officer is all right,' Lani would say. 'Isn't he, Vanda? Do you think he would do me outside of court?'

Vanda loved those times with Lani. 'We had,' she says, 'a lot of fun.' Hanging around Vanda I'd get starving for light relief, for harmless incongruities to show up the silly and the pompous about the way society does law and order—a young Vietnamese man Vanda was representing who bought coke for personal use only to discover the coke wasn't coke, it was salt, so he tried re-flogging the stash at Crown Casino. Whoever bought it off him called police and dobbed in the fake drug seller. I laughed and wondered if selling fake drugs was less illegal. A few months after that he died. Bad heroin had got on the streets again. I was looking for reasons to laugh, and they were out there, don't get me wrong, but death and grief were everywhere and like Vanda warned me no fairytales.

We were talking about Lani on our way to the Mint for a drink. The Mint is where William and La Trobe streets meet and as we neared the lights Vanda said: 'Last week, it was a lovely day, and just there, on that corner, was a dead body. A young man jumped off a building. Must have jumped off this roof here. I never noticed how high this building is.'

We looked up and, yes, somehow the building was much taller than you would register without looking up. 'His body was covered but you could still see an arm sticking out.' It passed unreported on the news. Media blackout. He was sixteen. 'I went home,' Vanda said, 'and posted on Facebook that we must look after our men. More men die in Australia from suicide than car accidents. Go home, I said—to your men, hug them, often they cannot tell you. Don't ask or expect them to tell. Just be there.'

Mike got a suspended sentence. Twelve months. 'We are grateful to the court,' said Vanda to the magistrate. Mike was bending over completely by then, head between his legs, it was lucky all in all, the snatching bit was too serious for Mike to be let off but the magistrate could have been scandalised, could have made his verdict sting. Though Vanda believes: 'A short, sharp sentence is no bad thing necessarily.' No reports were done on Mike. No one checked the possible implications of his mother, during pregnancy, having rubella, a condition linked to cognitive impairments that produced in Mike a flat ear at least and most likely a bunch of other troubles that stayed un-diagnosed—and no magistrate recommended court-integrated help services, chancing that they'd benefit Mike. Mike was slip-ping through the system. 'We don't have a system,' Vanda says, 'for people who don't fit. Our best hope is they learn how to live on welfare and not get involved with the criminal justice system.'

Except when you are poor and spend time on the streets, you'll get involved. You can get picked up for anything. For beg-ging or having weed or a Swiss knife on you. Mike breached his suspended sentence, went to jail, and Vanda dispatched a taxi to the caravan park where he'd been staying to collect his stuff and bring it to her St Kilda office. 'You have seen my of-fice.' No service exists for people jailed abruptly and wishing for their belongings to not disappear down a ditch.

One day, I think to myself, one day like this would be enough for me.

Ten years, thinks Vanda.

'Sometimes I wonder how much longer I can do it but then I think about everything I have gathered, relationships I have built, what a waste it would be. The thing about being em-bedded in the community, walking the streets, using the same public transport as my clients, not seeing people in my office, knowing people, knowing coppers, is I can connect people up and do something other lawyers cannot.' Time—lets trust stick, and relationships take anchor. 'So I think, surely I can do this for ten years.'

Vanda does not own a car. So, no Popemobile to cushion and escort her from one strife to the next. Most of Vanda's work is outreach. She walks a lot. I've also seen her stand without leaning on anything, back straight, two heavy bags hanging off a shoulder, for long stretches. It is not insignificant that she puts her body out there.

Not hiding is how Vanda does it.

It's a real issue, how to keep people real. And not make them into catchphrases for banners, appendixes to principles. Colleagues say Vanda understands her clients' lives and this is worth more than most things. Many who advocate on behalf of others don't want a connection with those they're advocating for. Aren't interested in talking politics. Twists and turns of human fate are not up for discussion. Whereas a smart lawyer who gets you, fights well for you, is like a doctor, the provider of an essential service.

For psychological stuff she sends people to Helen Barnacle, who was once jailed for heroin possession while pregnant and fought for her daughter to be with her until the age of four. One was the normal maximum allowable age. Helen got a BA inside prison. 'She is well known on the street, doesn't have a middle-class past,' Vanda says, 'doesn't go *oh, poor you!*'

Isn't easily shockable. NO FISHING. What does it take to not be shocked?

I hear one of Vanda's clients, homeless for now, sharply articulate, sum up the psychologists she saw before Helen. 'I don't mean to sound horrible but they were like textbooks. I would see the look of horror in their eyes.' Their eyes.

Perhaps one way of putting it is that many of Vanda's clients live their lives on a highway where they are repeatedly hit by passing trucks. As they are bandaging their wounds, cleaning them out with rainwater, putting bones back into sockets, another truck's oncoming. A backlog of injuries functions not unlike a backlog of grief, an expression I first heard near the desert in the Kimberleys where backlog describes the unrelenting holding of funerals on Aboriginal land, leaving the living no time to mourn the dead, creating an imploding paralysis. That is what's in the tar as well. Most people have a truck going over them at some period in their life. But on a highway you don't get one or two. You get a convoy. They don't stop. That's the point. The recurrence is the point. The point's the repetition.

'These middle-class people keep their cushy middle-class lives and my clients constantly have to be re-traumatised,' said Vanda after police charged (not her first charge-sheet appearance) Steph.

About the trucks: Steph was fifteen when she left home where her mother sexually abused her. Then in a foster home her carer, a married woman with kids, behaved in a way that to Vanda's ears sounded like studious grooming of Steph. No doubt it's hard with teenagers in care since being sexual is often the only way many can express affection or gratitude but not crossing lines is the carer's business. Once Steph came of age it turned into a full-fledged sexual relationship. Two maternal figures, one after another, betraying Steph, she lost her footing. That was the telling, typical thing: it was Steph who wasn't fine. After Steph left, the carer continued working with children, her family and employers none the wiser. 'The woman,' Vanda says, 'didn't behave illegally but she did behave amorally and gets to keep her family and money and nice life. What does Steph get to keep?'

When Steph was charged she was in hospital—distressed, smashed on valium, talking about wanting to kill her ex-carer. It was 2 a.m. with no prospect of Steph acting on her threats against the woman, who lived far away. Still hospital people called police. Later in court to explain Steph's behaviour Vanda had to bring up the sexual abuse. 'Where's the proof?' replied the magistrate. And added 'Anybody could say that.' Vanda was gutted. When Steph jumped up and screamed 'mate, she is a fucking pedodog' and the magistrate raised his voice in ordering Steph to sit down Vanda was gutted some more. The guy was silencing Steph in front of everyone as if no one ever learned the nature of kids getting abused is predicated on secrecy. On perpetrators feeling convinced nobody will believe victims and on their victims finding no space in which to speak of what happened. 'Sometimes I don't mind my clients getting a foot up their arses, this was not one of those times,' Vanda says. The suspended sentence Steph got was not the point. Once the magistrate opened his mouth it stopped being about sentencing.

That night—Friday—Vanda could not sleep. Kept going over everything. Could she have protected Steph, not mentioned the past? Not really. This magistrate's reaction was beyond anticipating. That weekend Steph tried, not her first attempt, to kill herself. Few things are worse than being disbelieved when the darkest stuff that ever happened to you creeps out to the open. New shame on top of the old shame, rage too, so urgent it wants to suck the bone marrow out of you.

Trucks, yeah, so. Sometime later Vanda noticed a newspaper make mention of a carer being investigated for inappropriate sexual relations. No name was given; Vanda was sure who. She popped the article in an envelope and posted it to Steph, a way of saying your experience is being taken seriously, you're not a liar or piece of shit. She's not aware if it gave Steph any relief.

I know Vanda's love is theatre but I prefer TV and this is how my mind works. If *Vanda*, the Scandinavian lawyers & cops psycho-thriller, went into development she'd be one of those in-demand street-literate females unscared of locking onto people's eyeballs once they've taken a hit, or even if no hit, not a gram, is to be had, shuttling between the world of the streets and the world of indoor-voice-only institutional spaces, brooding, marginally less broken than her clients: no. Vanda's sorted. You could attempt for TV script purposes drawing her as the conviction lawyer figure, the downtrodden's poster woman, but it wouldn't fit either while making dull viewing anyway so keep trying.

At the washing line next to the backyard sewerage puddle I'm joined by my neighbour. Just lost a best friend, young, fit, no known health troubles, to heart failure. He wasn't thirty yet; close to eight hundred made the funeral; they flew in, drove hours; he *touched*—is it pride in my neighbour's voice, a little opening deep in vocal cords dried out by shock?—so many. I think of the tiggy game my son plays at school. Someone who is 'it' chases and tags somebody who becomes 'it' and chases others. A version is played in every childhood. Those funerals for ourselves we imagined as children, and often way past being children if people who should have known better badly hurt us—they were crowded. And at those funerals we were 'it' because we were dead and we could run around and tag as many people as we liked with sadness. We could tag and couldn't be tagged. That's what being dead gave us.

Astrid's send-off was at Sacred Heart Church in St Kilda—
born 23.03.1985
died 21.12.2012

it said on the photocopied flyer, Vanda was wondering who'd come. When the start time arrived the pews were scattered with caseworkers and agency people. Lawyers: only Vanda. So that's what it would be like, Astrid farewelled by people who liked her and cared but were her paid minders (poorly paid, whatever) not kin. This was a sore point with Astrid, how people were paid to care about her, no one actually did. I never even met her. Something about the way Vanda invited me. I did not consider not coming.

Music first then Father John reads the eulogy by Astrid's adoptive mother, Maureen. She has not flown down from interstate. 'Astrid used to love music, used to love playing with the stereo knobs. She would twist the knobs and I would say "no". So she would stretch one hand to be slapped and with the other hand continue twisting.' The two-year-old lasted twenty-five more years, longer than many imagined. Her death was quieter than most would have guessed. How odd, she was usually careful with drugs, someone says. 'Astrid used to be the happiest, most cheerful, delightful baby. Then she hit the terrible twos, I used to joke she never got out of them.' Father John takes a breath. I picture a mother digging into her raw self for the image of a child, not doomed yet to become a tormented adult.

On the flyer's a photograph—Astrid sitting pretty, smiling,

right leg bent on the chair and you only see cuts on her arms if you know they're there. I place myself in front of another photo, which balances on a little church stand. Dark long hair. Athletic frame. Few people keep their looks after years on the street; this goes for women—self-evident?—more than men. Astrid stayed beautiful, beaming, the genes maybe, same ones that left Maureen powerless when trying to keep Astrid home, if you believe in them. She's in purple, her favourite. Ice skates. Once she was a teen ice-skating whiz at intermediate level of the Aussie Skate program. How photographs lie, this is known, the ones that age us, the ones peeling decades off faces like mudcakes off gumboots, this one at my eye level which makes Astrid's future look like it could save her from her past. What do photos' little lies matter? The dead are slipping away, all help's needed if we are to cling to the smallest parts of them.

Strange to be in a virtually deserted church on a January afternoon. The world feels OK, slow, out of our hands. City's a half-empty auditorium. Hot out I suppose. Too hot for memorial service clothes, even St Kilda style, unfussy. Astrid did not like clothes. She stripped, ran, police would call a local clinic connected to Alfred Hospital psych services and say 'a naked African-American woman is on the streets' and the psych people would go 'oh, yes, that's one of ours'. Vanda likes clothes. At the memorial service she is wearing black and red, one of her signature combinations. Every time she wears it, whichever season, it works. Hers is an old-fashioned glamour, Hepburnian (Katharine not Audrey). Katharine H compared herself to Campbell's tomato soup, savoury, no frills (must remember to ask what canned merchandise Vanda thinks she most resembles).

Don't forget the end of the day, Vanda said to me once. It's when community lawyers, social workers, agency people go home into beds while for others the search starts. That's when you glimpse the 'common humanity' figment coming undone. A death sometimes is like end-of-day writ large, people abandoned in their unadorned nakedness, stark loneliness, like in George Orwell's 'How the Poor Die'. The day she said it we were sitting drinking wine (hers red, mine white). Astrid was alive.

Father John is inviting people to say a few words. Only Vanda gets up. 'I admired Astrid's pluck, her guts, as well as being immensely frustrated by it. She had police, corrections and magistrates, everyone, wrapped around her finger, everyone playing her game.'

You dispense with the sad, limp air for a moment there, Vanda. You bring the friction back, the fight in the room.

'And I know we didn't completely fail her. There were moments of hope we gave her.' Vanda sits back down. Who was she just addressing—Astrid, Maureen in another state, herself, god who must not be totally indifferent when young raging women leave this world by accident or design? Father John reads from the prophet Isaiah about god removing the mourning veil, destroying death, wiping away tears (best translation this secular Jew can do) and afterwards, teas and supermarket biscuits in our grip, he tells me: 'People have tried lifting the veil for Astrid but ultimately death does it. Lifts that veil.' Death undoing the grief of living, I get it, I think. Vanda had mentioned Father John does funerals, a proper ceremony, for people with no relative even to come collect the body.

'I have studied the science of departures'—first line of Osip Mandelstam's 'Tristia'; and

> *who knows when the word 'departure' is spoken*
> *what kind of separation is at hand*

Mandelstam thought it was impossible to know. Vanda has lost enough clients, to drugs mainly but not only, to know the probabilities and likelihoods. She must have sensed Astrid was unlikely to make it. Still her death was shocking—sixty years premature, in another world. 'We all thought she'd die a more violent death. Suicide by cop.' Provoking police was not out of character for Astrid. 'Or something.' Vanda says she wanted to be in jail. 'Felt much safer there. She used to lie down under cars, too.' Two baby hands—one's twisting the knob, the other's offering itself for a ritual slap.

How wild, how angry, was she? Fiona at Alfred psych services was never scared of Astrid 'except this one time I went to the cells and she was there like an animal. Wanting to be put in jail. Out of control. She was terrifying.' Fiona's colleague Jacqui tells me Astrid wouldn't watch violent flicks, or open violent books, not ever, she liked 'soft stuff, soapies and weepies'. Vanda says Astrid's behaviour had hallmarks of sexual abuse—who, where, when, no one knew. She always went out of her brain around a certain time of year, her birthday, and invariably there'd be sexual overtones to it, her history of early abuse, whatever that was, being compounded by sex assaults that happened while working the streets and this stuff had to spill out some way, where? Whether Astrid's sharp mind—'insightful': Vanda—made things worse or better for her is unknowable. Vanda and Astrid would talk for hours in a space known as the Women's House. Astrid was doing a degree, indigenous studies were part of it, and she was interested in maybe one day expanding into law. To actually practise law—with her criminal record—what a miracle it'd be. They weren't kidding themselves Astrid in a white wig and robes was a chance, but they talked about how she should go get a law degree anyway, she could do a lot of good with it. 'I honestly thought I was going to win this one,' Vanda says. Something else won. Take abandonment, add abuse, then addiction, next mental health flare-ups. What do you get? Damage. Think again. She was an African-American without an African-American community. Family in America wanted nothing to do with her. So, what then? Loneliness. Of a cosmic kind. 'The alonest person I [that's Vanda] have ever met.'

A nearly unattended funeral. Whole person—gone—no one to be beside themselves with loss. Fingerprints on people and objects fade, become invisible, until it is as if they touched no one, nothing. Only their adoptive mother is feeling worse hourly. Fiona talked to Maureen—not inconsolable, but close—the day before the service. The mother does not have the daughter's anger. Just guilt. 'We've learned not to feel guilt in the interests of sanity,' Vanda says.

Just left the church and already I am forgetting. Like Astrid is a splinter of plywood and a river is taking her. River Lethe. River Time. All the talk about the sanctity of human life.

As if knowing your life is precious is a default state of the human psyche. As if everyone comes from this knowingness and always instinctively returns to it.

How about all those people for whom their life does not feel precious? Why not is often the easy bit to get: they were abused, abandoned, beaten to the point of forgetting they had a body, betrayed, humiliated, caught out by their socioeconomics like a mole in a spring trap. They were not loved or not loved enough. Lost someone, witnessed something, got into drugs or drink early, missed having their mental illness diagnosed, all of it, none of this. A harder question is can the feeling your life's worth shit be fixed, whether from outside in or inside out? Can it? All the services offering legal aid, food, counselling, employment (tedious employment), shelter, they cannot get close to this worth-shit feeling. I do not mean the needs they take aim at sit at the bottom of Maslow's pyramid (let's blow up the dumb pyramid). I mean this feeling's impervious to being messed with, it is too deep and diffused, a mystery even to its host, it is precognitive, it is metaphysical, both. And when this feeling is there it skews the survival instinct, instils that take-it-or-leave-it sense. Force of gravity's just too weak to pull you in. To keep you in. People, plans, debts, windfalls. Intangible stuff that holds you in—just not strong enough to stop you giving it away. 'The weightlessness of giving up.' I came across this expression in Kristina Olsson's *Boy, Lost*.

Some, maybe a lot, of this stuff comes from a place beyond us, from a time before we got born or can remember. How to speak of this beforeness? How to speak of things being passed on if they are not histories and habits so much as structures of feeling, also if it's unclear who or what is doing the passing on, plus why? *Cycles of abuse. Cycles of poverty. Intergenerational transmission of trauma.* Sorry, no can do, I tried and the words stuck in my throat.

Vanda has come to think those non-existent fairytale endings are always about the self-appointed rescuer, never the prospective rescue-ee. In *Vanda* the miniseries she wouldn't be raining redemption down on the heads of her co-star clients. Sunsets. Half-smiles of empowerment. Hope sweeter than flat lemonade in a jam jar. A Christmas not long ago she was crossing a park. She heard someone weeping—man, woman, at first she couldn't tell. It was a young woman thrown out by her boyfriend, abandoned by her family, on the streets for a few days, desperate, distressed. Takes someone with a special thickness of skin to walk past a crying person who has nowhere to go at Christmas. No, leave humanity out of it, Christmas too; Vanda being Vanda couldn't bear walking past. That day she was leaving for Tasmania to spend Christmas with the family of a man she was seeing at the time. 'Come on,' Vanda said to the young woman, 'let me buy you a coffee.' Everything was closed. So they went to Crown Casino. What the fuck was she doing? After coffee Vanda took the woman home—Vanda's home was a bedsit—feeling, she tells me, good about the idea of this young woman having a bath, food to eat, warm bed, books to read. Clean, fed, warm, safe. Everything Vanda would have wanted and needed. She left the woman at her place and got on the plane to Tasmania.

The man she was seeing thought she was crazy. Vanda called home. The woman did not pick up. When Vanda got back to Melbourne the place was deserted and everything in it not quite right. Mould in a coffee cup, days-old newspapers. The neighbours revealed the young woman's family had dragged her away. Later Vanda found out she threw herself off Jolimont Station railway bridge: didn't kill herself but broke every bone.

'I wasn't prepared to take all the steps.' This is what Vanda says and why, I realise now, she's telling me this story. 'I gave her what *I would have wanted*. But I wasn't prepared to give up my non-refundable flight to Tasmania and do things difficult for me—call counsellors from the Salvos, deal with mental health stuff…' Vanda says when we pick people up we are responsible for what we're doing and it is our responsibility to go all the way.

Says the fox in *The Little Prince* by Antoine de Saint-Exupéry: 'People have forgotten this truth but you mustn't forget it. You become responsible forever for what you've tamed.'

Does it mean a little help is often worse than no help? We're talking and I am getting a pulling feeling in my stomach. I get it when something important is happening and it's easy to miss. My body starts pulling on me from the inside. Vanda remembers a client going off at her for no good reason. This woman had a crime compensation claim taking forever to wind its way through the system in Alice Springs. Vanda's only part in it was making a couple of what's-going-on calls to the Alice Springs legal aid people. In the woman's eyes Vanda became the symbol of the obfuscating, stalling system. Usually Vanda's unshaken when clients get angry but 2009 was a bad year— it started with bushfires, then Vanda's best friend died from liver cancer—and she snapped. Gave it back at the woman. Shortly after that the woman was involuntarily committed. Again nothing to do with Vanda except she now knew that all along the woman was in serious trouble in her head. Later the woman killed herself, Vanda heard. 'And you ask yourself, perhaps if I didn't snap? Perhaps she was looking to me for hope?' This is not guilt of a whalehearted community lawyer talking. It's a dilemma and it's pressing, how to be in the presence of strangers who look like they may be sliding, falling, drowning and you just happen to be walking by, or seeing out of a corner of an eye some slippage, and if you've lived enough, tried one or two things, got your thermals wet maybe, you know obvious answers do not apply here and the likelihood of making things worse whatever you do is crushing.

Vanda and I both saw the *Australian Story* episode where a prominent rugby league player, first one out of the closet, tells of a troubled homeless boy he met on one of those hospital visits to sick kids that footy stars do especially the stars who are a soft touch. Years later as a teenager the boy lived with the player in a house he shared with a close female friend. The boy got off drugs, serious drugs they were, and went to school. He was safe and taken care of. After six months it emerged police were monitoring the boy because in the past he was seen entering houses of known paedophiles. The player, who had only recently come out—his dad begged him don't, and couldn't stop wishing his son was hetero—was a suspect. He got cleared fast enough and police asked him to pressure the boy to testify against the paedophiles who'd abused him. The boy knew enough to land key people behind bars. Most likely it wasn't burning desire for justice that got him talking. Maybe it was a way of repaying this famous sorted-out man whose respect he wanted. But testifying broke the boy. He stopped going to school, went back to drugs and older men. Homeless again. The player hardly ever knew where he was. One time police called the player after arresting the boy and the boy shouted wildly into the receiver for the player to get him out of there— this after months of no contact. The player had had enough. Had done so much for this boy, and for what? Any association now risked destroying him professionally. 'No, this guy is not my responsibility,' said the player to the cops. Four years later they found the boy's body: stabbed to death, wrapped in carpet, dumped in a shallow grave. Forensic reports suggested the murder was committed shortly after the player got the phone call. The boy's evidence could have brought down a paedophile ring so let's not be surprised by what happened to him. The player, tortured by the boy's death, dreams of replaying that phone call. Everyone around the player says not your fault, you did all you could, more even. The culture says it too. The man is beginning to believe it.

'I am sorry,' says Vanda, 'but it is your fault. You were to blame. I say it without judgment. You picked someone up and you expected a fairytale.'

A friend based in Cambodia for years who keeps going back—she's past eighty, it doesn't stop her—holds off clapping when another selfless young Australian sets up yet another orphanage in poor struggling Cambodia. 'Most of the children would only find a place in that orphanage because their parents have good connections,' my friend says. These are the small fries though. More worrying to my friend is that orphanage's likely proximity to higher-up corruption, to organised crime, proximity a selfless Australian can't see or foresee. It is not a question of charity and its corrosive ways in second and third world countries. My friend knows the damage that can happen when people force their way into complex ecosystems they do not understand.

Tempting to suppose a fragile, dysfunctional society isn't complex, can't satisfy its people's needs for meaning or a sense of self, and intervention can only help. Equally tempting to think a drug-taking boy who prostitutes himself to older men

and lives on the streets must be taken off streets because anything's better than the streets because the streets promise him
nothing but denigration and self-destruction. Except the idea
of human dignity isn't up to much if it does not encompass
recognition that people who look like they have little or nothing
may, in fact, have a great deal to lose.

Hang on—'All that is necessary for the triumph of evil is
that good men do nothing.' Is this not on every cereal packet,
Vanda? Meaning, don't block ears, avert eyes, speed up walking in response to another's cries. But what if the something
good men and women do is largely nothing masquerading as
a something, or if the something's worse than nothing because
it plucks people out of their own world then dumps them, with
fewer resources, less hope, once the good people collapse in
their inevitable moral exhaustion? Helping someone in unspoken expectation of their often impossible rehabilitation is frequently worse than not helping. Vanda has not always known
this, knows it now. It is a difficult knowledge. Would paralyse
me. What am I saying? It has paralysed me.

Take drugs. Vanda: 'Many lawyers and judges do not understand, or pretend they don't, that in telling people to give up
drugs they're asking them to give up friends, support, sense of
self, credibility, their way of spending time, everything.'

Even after climbing on top of addiction, like scaling a
mountain, only your two legs are in a sack, things may get
lonely or boring and how easy it is to slip. The time after rehab
or jail is dangerous. Easy to overdose and die: body cannot take
the usual doses. So when some or most retake up drugs it's not
like ring the village bells. Painful back and forth is how it goes.
In court one Tuesday, noticing deputy chief magistrate Popo-

vic's unmatronly air when she mentions kicking addiction, it's no breezy onwards-and-upwards business, I get goosebumps.

'Miss Popovic gets it,' Vanda's telling two young women who are up on shoplifting and loitering charges. Both women work the streets to support heroin habits. One was given heroin by her well-meaning mother when her ex, still living with her, moved his new girlfriend in. 'Use it, it'd make you feel better' said her mum and the young woman keeps saying 'I am so embarrassed' about the shoplifting: $144.20 worth of groceries. 'We are not talking about razorblades, cosmetics and deodorant. We're talking about food,' Vanda informs the court. The second woman, Ruby, has a prior conviction from a time of heavy drug use and is completing an advanced cookery diploma, favourite food Italian.

First Tuesday of the month is the Street Sex Worker List, held during afternoon hours to best fit with the women's nocturnal working life and in a separate court to avoid the perv factor. The hope is more women turn up and magistrates resist going ape on the women with fines that push them back trawling the streets so they can afford to pay the fines. Ruby pleads guilty—$998 in iPods and audio equipment that she converted into drugs. 'Despite the history, please consider a one-time no-conviction disposition,' Vanda says. She reckons Ruby is looking good, taking care, has had a number of clear urines. I sit back and wait for the lecture, the legal shit sandwich. 'I am amazed,' Popovic announces, 'at your perseverance, Ruby. On average it is ten withdrawals before a person succumbs to lifelong dependency or dies. You've had sixteen detoxes, two rehab stints, I don't think I've met anyone like you who just persevered. It demonstrates how hard it is. Despite your intelligence and commitment you're still relapsing.'

Did I hear respect expressed in a court of law for a woman who has gone back to drugs more times than Marina Abramovic invited a snake to orbit her head? Did she just call Ruby a 'remarkable young woman'? For every Popovic there may be a thousand morally squeamish sermon-makers, and for every Ruby there must be a metropolis of addicts who'll give up on giving up. But god what a mighty thing it is to see respect, a non-generic respect, given not because we all deserve respect as a matter of principle but because a young woman who turns up to court with sixteen detoxes in her bag deserves it specifically. I ask Popovic about respect. She says, 'Somebody said to me the other day, and I knew exactly what they meant, if you ask a seven-year-old what she wants to be no one is going to say they want to grow up and become a drug-addicted sex worker.'

Something happens between seven and seventeen, seventeen and twenty-seven. People's lives aren't straightforward. Society is only getting more complex, nearly every woe on the rise. The week before, we agreed to meet for coffee early. Popovic forgot. Too much was going on. I sat watching the cafe's open fire. Fantasised about being a lawyer. Better—a judge. I imagined a colossal sense of purpose. A tautness to my days. I imagined my words being like river embankments in the lives of people before me, preventing floods, redirecting the flow. Words of a writer are hardly worth a soggy biscuit most days. The week after, Popovic came on the dot, apologetic, not used to mucking anyone around. I asked her about dealing with people who feel trapped, about the tar, not saying 'tar' or wanting her to think me flowery. She has noticed among many young Aboriginal men a 'feeling like there is nothing, like they are trapped in their circumstances'. Sense of hopelessness converges with family obligations: you are expected to drink and go in that car, towards that bottleshop, licence or no licence, under the limit, over. An elder may say to a young man that a staunch man, for his family, is the better man. 'But because of stolen generations many people with a *broad* sense of family obligation do not have an *intimate* sense of family.' I ask Popovic about family. 'The effect of family can be devastating. I am now dealing with third-generation drug offenders.'

I was talking to the deputy chief magistrate and remembering all those famous physicists who, with each of their discoveries, gave birth to another generation of happy atheists while themselves moving closer to some form of faith, or at least towards a place of big doubt. Possibly science looked like the cleanest antidote to faith only for those sufficiently removed from science. I wondered if similar could be said about the law and order system, that the deeper in it you are, the antsier you get with lofty claims about justice and rehabilitation. Not because you're disenchanted, more because maybe—Rai Gaita's words—you have found a 'sorrowful sense of our vulnerability to affliction' to be a better guiding principle than 'let the punishment fit the crime'. Vulnerability to affliction, and also to chance, misfortune, genes, the family you are born into, postcode.

'Even if you were a cat, you wouldn't want to live there,' said the leading senior constable at Moorabbin Justice Centre to Vanda one overcast morning. *There* was a boarding house. *Cat* was in the constable's head because the grave of one, formerly the pet of a woman at the boarding house, was dug up by a fellow boarder. In the fight that followed, the alleged grave-digger was hit with a mug, suffering a gash on her forehead, the dead cat's owner claiming self-defence since the victim, as she put it, had a spade. In the prosecutor's file I saw close-ups: a spade, a gash, a mug. 'I sometimes say to my clients,' Vanda said to the constable, 'if police arrived at a different time, the accused would be the victim and the victim the accused' to which the constable agreed 'oh, yes, often this is how our mind works. Whoever comes to us first we end up thinking of as victims.' Vanda's clients coming to police or to anyone—that's rare. Fear of being charged over some forgotten or unforgotten breach is too strong.

At Collingwood Neighbourhood Justice Centre, Vanda is there to see Georgie, who's transgender, only Georgie fronted up the day before—got the date wrong. Wanting to sort out a victims of crime matter, Georgie was told instead they were expecting her the next day to deal with a breach of community corrections orders. Also hanging over Georgie are charges pertaining to possession, prescriptions forgery, forgery of cheques. Most of these she disputes, all of them she could have settled seven years ago, if only she'd come to court.

Georgie is not here. Vanda calls her. *Where are you, Georgie? If you are on Collins Street, what's the problem with hopping on a tram and coming here? Get this sorted then you can get your victims of crime stuff happening too.*

('Pretty sage, Vanda,' says Beth from Corrections, listening in, 'I won't say it's particularly ethical but it's pretty sage.')

No, Georgie, you won't be put in jail. No. We have to deal with this stuff today. Just come. [quiet] *No, Georgie, you can't do it on your own timetable. You have to come when they tell you to come. You cannot in-*

definitely avoid dealing with this. You'll be picked up and put on remand. [quiet] *I can adjourn it for two weeks but what guarantee do I have you'll show up?* [quiet] *No, I cannot hang around here all day.*

('She is not coming,' Vanda mouths to Beth from Corrections.)

People flunk court orders, miss court appearances, miss drug or alcohol counselling sessions, each missed step increasing the missteps for which they must be penalised. 'They may say yes and may even believe they'll do it, turn up, but there is no way,' Vanda says. Better, she thinks, to get a suspended sentence and be done, no permanent headspin in the rehabilitation maze, less contact with the system. 'Don't forget, if cops want to get narky with trans people they can put them in cells or remand centres with men.' Terror of that annihilates other impulses. It produces a blanket avoidance. Which in turn gets punished. Sooner or later the system must flare impenetrably hostile on Georgie.

Must be naive—of course I'm naive because it still surprises me every time the justice system, even at its most banal and procedural, is a trap. The ground opens up and chomp, chomp, chomp goes the ground. Once she's down in the system's sublayers it is already too late for Georgie to get support. Others too, be they more obviously functional, or differently yet equally interestingly dysfunctional, if the justice system treats you with dignity the outside world still won't. 'Nobody should be punished beyond what court determines. But society,' Vanda says, 'punishes people.'

Mike, Lani, Steph, Ruby, Georgie—can't imagine them ever being part of the festivities, seated at society's table, eating buttered crumpets with fork and knife. And Astrid? She's taken care of the answer to that question.

Tracy is murdered in a broken-down white Econovan parked on Greeves Street opposite the Gatehouse, a safe space for St Kilda streetworkers. She lived in the van with Tony, her boyfriend, minder. They had been together a long time, loved each other. People talk about Tracy in something like unison, they say sunny, gorgeous, impeccably polite, interested in others, warm; she stood on her corner—she had her own corner—so dignified. Her back straight. The best posture. 'When I saw her I'd stand straighter,' someone says. She was classy. While knowing the dangers. Tony looking out for her was a plus.

'Tracy's murder,' Vanda emails me, 'scared the women. That hasn't lasted long though. Desperate people are out there, need for drugs outweighs fear.'

Tony and Tracy had broke away from St Kilda, clean at last, they were living with Tony's mother, taking care of her when she got sick. Her death pushed them back. They restarted on heroin, money ran out, eventually, reluctantly, they returned. Tracy by all accounts hated being out on the street again. Tony was in hospital when Tracy got killed. He found her. The murder was brutal. I won't supply you with details. Police think it could have been a client and are working on a robbery-gone-wrong scenario but the killer is on the tear and it's been years. Interpol's involved. Tony has collected the car numberplate numbers of more than three thousand of Tracy's clients in her last eighteen months. If he'd been with her in St Kilda and not having a major infection treated (Tracy made him go) none if it would have happened (got to live the rest of his life with that).

Tracy's death is linked in the media to that of Jill Meagher, not a sex worker, an ABC radio employee from Ireland, who didn't work the streets but was walking home along one after drinks with colleagues. Adrian Bayley, who raped and killed Jill five hundred metres from her Brunswick home and sleeping husband Tom, had to his name, among other convictions, sixteen rapes in under a year against St Kilda sex workers. That's how many on record. So the real number could be anything. In an interview I saw, a woman at a strip club Bayley frequented said he was violent and a total freak but hardly the only one. When Jill was killed, thirty thousand marchers protested street violence, enough flowers piling up near the bridal boutique where CCTV cameras last filmed Jill that council workers were called in and removed them. Sea of flowers equals traffic hazard. Ten months later, it was Tracy, to the corner where she'd stood—it's Tracy's Corner now—people brought with them flowers, candles, letters and banners, and a clear sense that seeing as Jill's death provoked an outcry Tracy's couldn't be ignored. On Greeves Street a candlelight vigil was planned, the publicity posters saying

She is Someone

A peaceful gathering to remember Tracy

which annoyed me. Someone? Was her humanity ever really in question? At a separate big memorial service a banner said WOMEN OF ST KILDA SUPPORT THEIR SEX WORKERS. 'Fucking thank you,' said Vanda who skipped the service and went instead to an all-nighter at the Gatehouse, where everyone who was gathered knew Tracy and Tony.

We don't need to say it. Both of us think about Astrid's service.

We don't need to say it but actually we say it after a few drinks (white = me, Vanda's = red)—say something in the rhetoric around Tracy's death didn't sit well. I have no right to a position, not that it ever stops me. I mutter something about things feeling wrong. 'Felt forced,' Vanda says, 'contrived.' Didn't feel like it was about Tracy. It was about a principle. About an idea. Which is fine. Important. Good that it happened and, who knows, perhaps in all of this someone's life was saved but it was not about Tracy. Or Tony. When Jill died people said *could have been me, my daughter, my sister, my girlfriend.* After Tracy's murder some were trying to say the same about her. Others, especially online, countered that heroin-injecting hookers with even the most lovable foibles are not us. It was not quite *she had it coming* but not that far off.

Curious thing: empathy via identification. If we say it could have been me, shouldn't we first ask who was she? And wouldn't the answer to that usually take aeons of decoding? And what if Tracy couldn't have been me and I couldn't have been Tracy (I never for instance had an addiction of the kind that would make me again and again, for years, do things I hated doing)? There's much that's not known about others and much of it is unknowable. What can be grasped of another person's suffering has limits. Ignore the limits and people become symbols, vessels in which we carry liquids of our choosing. Things—whereas to recognise another person as fully human is also to notice what in that person is different, and to not twist the difference into near-saintliness. On the street as anywhere, people are good and bad, both at once. Poverty, neglect, abuse or disadvantage—people's pasts do not coat them in fairy dust or make their actions always already morally defensible. If we feel roused only when picturing people as morally elevated by their misfortune then ... well. Beyond sad.

When going to sleep Vanda sometimes imagines an avalanche of snow dropping on Melbourne. She imagines bringing people in to where she is, giving them food, turning cold away. She doesn't think about what happens later. Just the sheltering. Then she falls asleep. 'All we can do is smooth a bit a very hard road,' she said to me after a morning in court of applying for adjournments, community service orders, no-conviction dispositions. Most of the people would be back within months for the same sorts of thing and she would represent them again and it wouldn't feel Sisyphean, not to her. She was rolling rocks out of their way, didn't matter that the rocks roll back. 'People have hard, hard lives and you just make a little bit easier their life that is damn hard. Mind you,' she says, 'I have clients say *it was never meant to be like this. I went to Brighton Grammar.*' Cushy lives fall apart too. (Watch out.)

Kierkegaard wrote hope is 'a new garment, stiff and starched and lustrous' and recollection 'a discarded garment that doesn't fit' though it was beautiful once, exquisite, while repetition is 'an indestructible garment... neither binds nor sags'. Repetition, like recollection, may suggest a tilt back in time (*re*play, *re*load, *re*wire, *re*voke, *re*pent) but for Kierkegaard repetition's movement is always towards the future, into 'the new', it is the state of being inside time. He thought while Greeks taught us all knowledge is recollection, 'modern philosophy will teach that all life is a repetition'.

Some years ago one of Vanda's clients was utterly determined Vanda should sleep with her. The woman sent cards to Vanda c/o the St Kilda legal branch, toys too, which began to stack up at reception. 'Is it your birthday, Vanda?' She was refusing to open the cards but couldn't send them back as the woman's current address was unknown. An experienced case-worker had once advised Vanda, if a client propositions you don't say 'oh no, how unprofessional, I mustn't because of my job' or 'no I can't, I have a partner' because the client may take it the job or partner is the obstacle and, were this obstacle removed, you'd sleep with them. You have to say a firm no at the outset. Vanda had another client walk with her to the office from a clinic at St Kilda Junction. This woman was talking rather insistently about the two of them getting a room in a motel, no one need find out, and Vanda was saying 'look, this is a bit unprofessional' and doing her best to be firm but still respectful. They said their goodbyes. Vanda got inside. Pulled out her phone. Almost instantly a message beeped. 'And who said you were professional anyway?'

Vanda couldn't stop laughing. She tells me the story and we are laughing together. What a good feeling to laugh like this. Such freedom in it. We're like a pair of balloons out in the sky (not helium, not us) pushed further into the atmosphere by wind and cold air. When it is time we will return to earth as little bits of balloon spaghetti. Learned articles tell me we will freeze up there first. That's OK with me. With you, Vanda? 'While we do know that animals occasionally eat these soft slivers of rubber,' I read, 'the evidence indicates the pieces ultimately pass through the digestive system without harming the animal.'

PART TWO

I've heard Lorrie Moore say in a lecture she delivered at New York Public Library that parenting's mostly useless: in the making of personhood the culprits are biochemistry and residential zipcode. Her lecture was entitled Watching Television, something Moore and her three siblings were more or less banned by their parents from doing on moral and religious grounds. Prohibition produced in them neither a great uniform hunger for TV's pleasures nor uniform contempt for TV's distractions. Instead came four zigzag reactions, four lives in which TV was not important or unimportant, which for Moore was more proof of parenting's small role and the big role of other things, chiefly postcode, easily obscured in the 1.8-meets-2.2-kid families world. All that's needed, Moore said, is a large enough sample and we will see most people become who they need to whatever their parents get up to.

I was thinking the opposite. Somehow something claims us. Certain prototypes assert themselves, usually later in life. And for those who took an oath a long time back to (I do not count myself in this group) under no circumstances become our parents this may feel like a form of possession, or like being possessed. You open your mouth and your mother's voice comes out complete with your mother's words. Stuck in a mirror's that old inbuilt irony: your father's eyes. It's like Mikhail Bakhtin's idea that every utterance in this world contains in some way all the utterances that preceded it. We contain our parents, doesn't mean we are them, it means we go from being inside of them to them being inside us.

Hungarian writer Péter Esterházy wrote an 850-page novel at the beginning of our century—the 21st, which did you think?—called *Celestial Harmonies*. That's the English translation, the book was in part a tribute to his father who was a count by birth, member of a prominent Austro-Hungarian clan, a man stripped of everything by the new communist government at WWII's end and forcefully relocated to the countryside. He stayed an aristocrat in spirit, and in his admiring son's eyes. ('My father never looked down on anyone, which is how he was an aristocrat. My grandfather looked down on everyone, which is how he was an aristocrat. As for me, I just keep blinking.')

Celestial Harmonies was divided in two. In Book One paternal ancestors spanning centuries were referred to as 'my father'; in Book Two 'my father' was his actual biological father, Mátyás. The idea of Book One's 'my father' including all the fathers of all the family's sons—a conceit aided by the Esterházy clan's fame but just as apt, I feel, for us dynastic pipsqueaks of no spectacular lineage—collided with the recent history of communist dictatorships sabotaging familial bonds. Lenin, Stalin, plus other minor Soviet bloc dictators whose inner workings I know less about, were heralded as their people's true fathers ('oh lord, You are our Father, we are the clay and You our pot-

ter'—that was the verbatim thrust of it, or verbatimish, in our
godless lands). In our big father's name we were supposed to
be ready to denounce our little fathers and grandfathers. State
trumped family. Family was treacherous. Who's your daddy?
Think before you answer.

Almost by accident after his father's death Esterházy discovered that Mátyás, a man presumed unmuddied by the regime's filth, was in truth an informer. Never went beyond being
an amateur informer, he developed no taste for it, no knack,
but he clocked in regularly and, as Esterházy has remarked
in one interview or another, it would be ethically vacuous to
suppose the reports his father delivered to his handlers, usually during soccer matches the father attended with the son,
times the son always regarded as their special time together,
could ever be harmless. These things never were. How things
turned for the son was he was writing another book, a thin
one, about requesting the files to see who'd informed on his
father—Mátyás with his blue blood seemed a sure target in
communist Hungary—only to run into the names and lives of
those his father informed on. *Revised Edition* never got trans-
lated into English. Not enough daughters and sons of the anglophone world discovering their parents were informers and
notions they hold dear about their family and selves, along with
a swag of childhood memories, are in need of revision? Who
knows why *Revised Edition* didn't make it to English. I read it in
Russian. Gulped it down. Then I read a Russian critic, Grigory
Dashevsky, describe the thing that Esterházy in black and red
coloured type is doing:

He is not dissociating himself from his father... He is expelling, virtually belching out his father from himself—and then he is attempting to reattach himself to his father in desperate or mocking comments addressed to him.

Red for his father's words in the reports to his handlers, black for Esterházy's own reaction on reading them. Often his reactions are abbreviations, jottings: 'tears', 'self-pity', 'i.o.t.m.' (it occurs to me), 'I imagine'. His is not a pushing away of a parent in shame and disgust followed by a pulling that body back, a pained, partial re-embracing. It is precisely *belching out* your father then re-submerging him inside yourself. We contain our parents just the same if they betray themselves or us.

Tackling (someone has to) the dirty dishes pile I catch a talkback program about compulsive hoarding on the radio and a man rings in with a voice that could be in its forties, might be in its sixties: 'I have my parents to thank for my compulsive hoarding. They survived the Depression and it was ingrained in them. And here I go too.'

This is the story sentenced to constant retelling, about how people are born into things, and fate thinks intergenerationally. Parental pain, sadness, abuse (be it suffered or inflicted), indifference, withheld love, riding and exploding over children's lives, like tanks.

Borges's Infinite Library of Larkin's they-fuck-you-up-your-mum-and-dad fables.

No subject's more without an end than this. Us and our parents, it dogs us, even taking away the spectre of historical catastrophe or a private catastrophe, as if the catastrophe kinds can ever be mutually exclusive. Lush fog shrouds what gets passed on between parents and children. Fog of too much meaning, too many excavated parallels.

More echoes than in an echo chamber!

More cause and effect than in a closed-loop electrical circuit!

And that's without touching on killing the father or marrying the mother and all the inexhaustible variations. This overproduction of meaning, the overdetermined feel of it, is I guess what Lorrie Moore objects to. She's asking how much parents need to tell themselves they're the potters and their children the clay. How else to sustain a lifetime of devotion and sacrifice if not through a self-seeding delusion of your importance? As for children aren't they always on the lookout for alibis, and once they become parents, is it so inconceivable they'd get co-opted into the machinery of self-delusion? Philip Roth—*Portnoy's Complaint*—

> The legend engraved on the face of the Jewish nickel—on the body of every Jewish child!—not IN GOD WE TRUST, but SOMEDAY YOU'LL BE A PARENT AND YOU'LL KNOW WHAT IT'S LIKE

—writing specifically about Jewish parents' hold over their children in post-WWII America, and writing not specifically at all.

I have great parents. Great Jewish parents. My parents occupied a large space in my life growing up but they never loomed. I was reminded of this while reading Karl Ove Knausgaard describe the relationship with his father. His father who loomed. *Whether he hit me or not made no difference. It wasn't the pain I was afraid of, it was him, his voice, his face, his body, the fury it emitted, that was what I was afraid of, and the terror never let up, it was there for every single day of my entire childhood.* I can remember no instance of being seriously frightened of my parents. Surely freedom from this fear is one of the most important facts about me and my life. Here is another. When we immigrated I was a teenager and never in danger of replicating, unwittingly or otherwise, my parents' lives. The country we left collapsed shortly after and the one we found ourselves in showed little resemblance to anything my parents knew or had the paints to paint. So, free, that was me. Unlike many non-first world migrant parents pushing their children to succeed lest the children feel the shame of being nobodies in a land where they have zero social and emotional infrastructure—lest the children, too, be forced to in other words (not my parents' words) eat shit—my parents stayed unwavering in respecting my autonomy. Without most likely realising it, they released me from serving the family's need for self-affirmation and survival, each family consisting not only of the living but of its dead and its yet-to-be-born.

They say you start noticing signs (i.e. of channelling your parents) once you have your own children but I had my first child by myself, and being a single parent, another experience foreign to my parents, in a country which worked by laws that to us still felt largely unfathomable, freed me again. Or maybe I was simply too young and full of self-devised commandments, very much 'in my head' about what kind of mother I was going to be, not worn out by life either and, also, grateful for my parents' parenting and unhellbent on opposing them. (Knausgaard has four children—'With them I have tried to achieve

only one aim: that they shouldn't be afraid of their father.')
Free from slavish re-enactment or repudiation of family scripts,
I could observe myself being my parents' daughter. Sometimes
my parents would poke out of me like legs out of a pregnant
belly. Sometimes they were white noise filling me from the inside and jamming all other sounds, making room for a disqui-
eting silence. I don't mean to make too much of my freedom.
It's always been provisional and partial. Still, the longer I live,
which is to say the more arcs of other people's lives I glimpse,
the more astounding this freedom looks to me.

One day I was talking to Lisa and all the way I had Katie
and Bryn in my head then we moved on to families. Lisa said,
'Suicide in a family is like a cross on your forehead,' and I had
no idea until that moment that both her father's siblings committed suicide. For decades she believed that was going to be
her too. Lisa was about the last person I expected to hear these
words from. She seemed to me free of deep self-destructive
urges, what would I know, turns out in her thirties Lisa would
go to sleep with an image of blowing her head off. It came
from outside of her. She could not make it go away. This story,
its forcefield, was theirs, not hers, still something, a feeling like
being marked maybe, stuck to her. Till it stopped eventually.
It's like she grew out of it.

As soon as Lisa told me this my ears opened and I started hearing others speak of the cross on the forehead. Where
was I, or it, before? Flicking the kitchen radio on one morning to keep me and the tabletop debris company, I listened
to American writer David Vann talk, and never before had I
heard anyone be so open about a parent's suicide with strangers whose faces he couldn't see. I got obsessed with Vann, read

all he wrote, downloaded every interview I could find. He was thirteen when his father took his life. Ashamed of the truth he'd tell people his father died of cancer. And he burned with a feeling he would repeat his father's fate. It would happen like this: he'd hit a low point and 'suicide would just be waiting for me'. Vann said, 'For twenty years I had a feeling of doom. That's the only word for it. The full Anglo-Saxon meaning of it. Things would be bad, I would get depressed, and it would be unstoppable. I believed it.'

Then he hit a low point. Things were bad enough he thought here it comes. And … he found he had no desire to kill himself, that's what it took for him to finally be free. To get there and to see for himself.

Twenty years—apparently psychologists and psychiatrists, I've asked a few, hear it a lot, a suicide in a family can open a door best left shut and then if the winds are strong enough and persistent enough the door may flap menacingly, invitingly, could be both. The flapping door, responsive to wind, is nothing like the fictitious 'suicide gene'. When Nicholas Hughes, son of Sylvia Plath, killed himself that gene du jour did headline overtime in the dumber media outlets. And it is less bureaucratic feeling than 'contagion'. Still I cringe. The straining, clumsy language at our disposal to encapsulate what a suicide may leave behind feels like a stand-in for the real language to come. We wait, twist our necks right and left, but the real language is not here.

I want to know about the cross and the forehead. To be haunted and shaped by a parent's anguish is one thing. To be doomed to repeat it no matter the life you have made for yourself? A vision of a child locked into a parent's death won't leave me alone. Something to do with the past asserting itself across generations as destiny, a choicelessness stemming not from the big geopolitical stuff of dispossession, persecution, trauma but from forces below skin no one has a grip on. The soul of another—its ills, its deepest needs. The webs families weave. (Plus genes.) Also the real possibility Heraclitus was more right than wrong in proposing 'a man's character is his fate'. In some interview—he's done a gazillion—Knausgaard gets asked what he thinks of fate. He replies no one believes anymore in fate. It's dead. An outdated concept. Yet aren't we, he adds, the same human beings who were here ten generations ago? What happened to those things we knew to be true? Where'd they go?

Nowhere. Inextinguishable—even in this world lit by the fires, or so we've been assuring ourselves, of our unassailable free will.

I always thought, a commonplace thing to think, nothing could be worse than parents losing their children and now I'm slapped with children left behind by their parents. Left behind by. And with—this feeling, can't be shaken off or willed away, of being bound to replicate their parent's final act; don't call it choice, it's at least some of the time much more complicated than that.

Amanda—we meet to talk about Stephen from Bryn's school but the conversation goes where it needs to go—introduces me to Martin.

Martin was twenty when his father killed himself. Now that he's double that twenty feels young. It didn't then. He thought he was old enough to cope: the second oldest, three sisters and him, four kids under five at one point. 'Mum said Dad was OK when we were babies.' By the time they were children then adolescents the dad was a long way from OK. Down and absent emotionally, he was also angry, paranoid. Also jealous of his wife especially if she was out with friends. Martin's parents' rows spilled out to the street. Loud, violent—everyone heard. Martin's best friend could definitely hear. He lived next door. Martin boiled with shame at those times. But to hope his parents might split up? That would be worse than their marriage's public unravelling. Martin tells me, 'Mum used to come to me when I was eight or nine and say should I go back to him? I remember it clearly, her asking me. I didn't want the shame of my parents splitting up. I would tell her to go back.'

They lived in a small town in England's north. When things got out of control the kids went to grandparents close by. After a few days they'd return and it'd be quiet. Devout Catholic family. The kids saw it this way: their mother, the most amazing mother in Martin's eyes, was good, innocent and their father bad, the evil husband and dad. Martin was scared of him despite only being hit by him once or twice. 'Much later I realised Mum was quite provocative. Spoiling for an argument. I'd wish she'd just keep quiet.' Martin came to see his mother was not emotionally there for the kids, though she looked after their physical needs, and his father did love them and care for them in his way. He loved nature. Took them on fantastic holidays—luxury of luxuries, lots of Martin's friends didn't go anywhere ever.

'I really withdrew in childhood, right into myself, had real problems relating to men, older men in particular.' School was difficult. College was 'three years of hell'. It never got easy. 'I spent my whole life being a good boy, which is really hard to do. Because you can't be good all the time. Every time I wasn't good, in my eyes I was terrible.' Wanting to be good also means you don't get to find out who you really are. Martin still has problems finding work, staying in jobs. 'I think if somebody's angry they're angry at me. I may have absolutely nothing to do with it but it feels personal.' Living like that's exhausting. There is only so much fear-produced adrenaline coursing through your body and head you can take. His dad died three or four months after Martin moved out to go to college. 'Things turned really bad when I left. Mum moved into my bedroom then to a flat.' Martin's father went to live with his parents which was where he drowned himself. Martin's sisters rang with the news.

Martin got on the train, numb, no tears came. The funeral was terrible. His dad's parents were blaming the wife and kids for their son's death. 'And we were with Mum's side of the family who were going on about what a bad person Dad was. So you couldn't really grieve.' The funeral came, went and Martin still hadn't cried. No one in his family made an outright agreement after that to not mention the suicide, it just happened that way. 'You get quieter and quieter about it.' It took years of telling no one and it doesn't jump out of his mouth now but, when it's right, he is OK with talking about it.

He used to drive along wanting someone to crash into him. The option of suicide was already stolen by his dad. 'How bad would I have to be to do to the people who love me what my father did to us?' He doesn't blame his father and as he gets older he's understanding him more. 'The greatest difficulty I have had is feeling I will inevitably fail at the same things.' Same things include: being a husband, a father, reining anger in, finding a place for himself in the world, stopping shame and depression sucking life and hope out of relationships. He says 'it's the most fundamental thing in life, your parents' and if they are there but not really there that's the worst, because you keep coming to them for support, protection, acknowledgment then when it's knocked back something in you recoils further from the world. Each year even if this stuff is not explicitly in his head he gets morbid, and when he wonders why the world's feeling that way sometimes it takes his wife to say, 'It's the anniversary of your dad's death.'

I ask about feeling bound, what that feeling feels like.

'On occasions I have a fleeting sense I am him and I am seeing the world through his eyes. Sounds weird I know but his presence is impossible to avoid. I think it's always going to be with me. I will never be over it. Something I've realised, or have realised I'd realised, or re-realised, is I look like my dad—I can see my dad out the corner of my eye if I catch my reflection. I couldn't look in the mirror for years and years because of the resemblance. And I'm sure the shame... I think he was pretty ashamed as well. I only look in the mirror to do my shaving. There are always images in your head anyway of what you look like and how the world sees you and I've looked out imagining the world looking back at me as my dad... You find yourself trying to rearrange the way you're looking. So people are not thinking you're a threat.'

The way he's better now, freer, is this: he has had a child and is a good father to her although he needs to watch himself. His wife has stayed, even though they separated then got back together and it's been touch and go many times and she is weary as hell. They love each other. She fought for him. Amanda is part of the fight. This repeating business is not written in some stars or on tablets alongside the commandments. It has taken him this long, the freedom he has scratched out for himself is this fragile, because the other thing is lodged that deep. Most likely his wife saved him. He no longer thinks he has no choice. And he does not want to die, his father's way or any way. We say goodbye, rushing, he to his child and I to mine. I don't have a feeling of a happy ending (though I know Martin alive, a father, a husband, is as happy as it gets) because it seems to me heartbreaking that a man should spend four decades of his life trying to pull himself apart from his father's life then death.

I ask psychiatrist Paul Valent about the cross on the forehead. We're meeting to talk about child Holocaust survivors, he is one himself—but the conversation's duck-diving where it needs to dive to and I'm telling him about Lisa, Martin, David Vann.

And Valent's saying, 'It applies to illness as well, people believing they have the illness their parent died from when they get to their parent's age. Or them *actually having it* and dying at that age. Same happens,' Valent says, 'with older siblings dying and younger siblings reaching the age of their sibling's death then having an accident.' I read an interview with Robyn Davidson, an Australian writer, eleven when her mother killed herself; she did not dwell on it obsessively nor imagine herself fatally marked. 'I don't recall that I suffered any sort of guilt, or grief. Then when I hit forty-six, which was how old she was when she died, boy, I got the whammy.' Decades of nothing then ambushed. An ambush rather than a hover. I speak to a woman who lost her sick mother as a child but marched herself through the rest of school, followed by university (first in her family to go), next a career in the public service, then she hit her mother's age—a weakness she couldn't shrug, undefinable by doctors, mystery affliction. She took months off work and lay in bed.

'There is chronological time,' Valent tells me, 'and there is experiential, cyclical time. This time has an emotional meaning. Existential. It is like the way peasants think about harvest: time to reap and time to sow. Time to live and time to die.'

At the Museum of Old and New Art in Hobart I wait for people to go away and I stand in front of Anselm Kiefer's *Sternenfall/Shevirath ha Kelim*—falling stars, the breaking of the vessels, it translates as. Most of the museum is without natural light. But the pavilion built to house this one sculpture of Kiefer's has floor-to-ceiling windows on two sides. A glass passage leads into it. More light. 'Kiefer demands pavilions so he's going to get his fucking pavilion,' is MONA boss David Walsh's attitude. The work is four spilling-out rows of giant books made of sheets of lead, and interspersed between lead pages are jagged glass panes that look like they may fall and shatter on the floor, where shards of glass already lie, surrounding everything, as if the falling and breaking of glass is unstopping, cannot stop. On some of the shards are engraved the long astronomical numbers NASA scientists give to stars.

Breaking of the vessels is a concept from the Kabbalah. In the course of creation god poured divine light into ten vessels but the vessels proved not strong enough to contain the light and most shattered. Sparks of light were trapped in the vessels, countless fragments of which fell down into the realm of matter, which is how evil and discord entered our world which, said scholar and rabbi Adin Steinsaltz, is 'the worst of all possible worlds in which there is still hope'. (Also: it is the best of possible worlds because it carries within itself the chance of repair and redemption.) As always with Kiefer, semi-recent history infuses his scene of mythical world-making. Oversized lead books that have the appearance of being made from ash—reminder of the burning of books; broken glass—Kristallnacht.

For a few minutes no people are around. It is not my first time seeing the work. Won't say I'm transfixed—too baroque—but I am something. I am rearranged. Kiefer's words come into my head. 'I am against the idea of the end, that everything culminates in paradise or judgment.'

So this is how it is, I think. Stars rain from the sky like shards of glass. Time makes room for timelessness. Creation is always a catastrophe, a shattering. Everything has already happened. The past does not move through the present like a pointed finger or a shadowy confessor in a long cloak. The past is not *told you so*. Not *this is how it all began*. It is a knock on the door in the middle of the night. You open the door and no one is there. You cannot tell yourself it must be those feral boys from the corner house because it is too late even for them, and no you could not have heard the knock in your sleep because you've been wide awake all night like a hermit crab. So this is how it is. Stars fall from the sky like shot baby sparrows in Mao's China. Books are imperishable only because turning them to ash takes so little (it's not like blowing up buildings); they are imperishable only because they are so ready to survive, dispersed across the world, as trails of dust, kernels, memories, shreds. As to us, me and you, oh it's simple. We are the broken vessels containing, spilling all over the place, those who came before us.

PART THREE

In a Russian town situated —— k's outside Moscow some high
school students found the diary of a young man from the generation of boys WWII mowed down. This same generation,
born in the late 1910s, or early 1920s, dead by 1945, existed
in most European countries but in the Soviet Union—'Die but
do not retreat' (J. Stalin)—it left behind a demographic black
hole. The students brought the diary to school. It had an aura,
an authentic historical document, doubly compelling for being not ensconced in some library or archive. They'd rescued
it from almost certain obscurity. That made them care more.

The diary belonged to a young man who in 1937, the peak
of the Great Terror, joined the NKVD 'secret police' school
where elite cadres were trained to expose enemies of the Soviet
state. A million and a half such enemies were arrested, more
than 700,000 shot, and three months into his studies, under-
taken with zeal, the young man's parents got scooped up for
being exactly the anti-Soviet elements their son was trained to
eliminate: spies, terrorists, saboteurs. As befits the son of enemies of the people, the young man was promptly and without

any unnecessary sensitivity expelled from the NKVD school. This was how it worked (the West learned it from *The Gulag Archipelago*): the nearest relatives of found enemies were not simply a pitiful handful of shocked family members, they were the wife of an enemy, mother of an enemy, child of an enemy, each in their own right enemies. The diary ended at WWII with the son doing the one thing he and his severely contaminated social DNA were still allowed to do: he died while defending his country.

Was the diary's aura this, a young man's universe of meaning, and his parents, both cancelled at a stroke? This young man who desired nothing more than to be the littlest cog in the system was crushed with categorical indifference by that system. How many true believers were swiped away this way and died in camps and in front of execution squads still shouting or whispering Comrade Stalin! or The Party! or Our Great Embattled Motherland! and other vintage true believer slogans? And many, many of them must have thought that the purges were a mistake, that the party was infiltrated by fascists, that the true ideals (worth dying with a song for) were being subverted. And in a sense even though he escaped both the camps and the firing squads (for that he would have, if he could have, had the war to thank) the young man was just another faceless, loyal child munched up with no second thought by his motherland.

The students turned the diary into a play and staged it at their school. The spell was cast, particularly on the young man playing the main character, so enraptured was he that he wrote a paper about the diary and its author for a nationwide history competition instigated by Memorial, a human rights society. (Should the Memorial competition sound like one of those well-intentionedly meaningless civic initiatives to get schoolkids to care about something or other, keep in mind it has been going since 1999, is coordinated by Irina Sherbakova, a world-class historian of the Soviet twentieth century, and attracts three thousand papers annually and especially from the regions and provinces. Most submissions do the hard historical work of uncovering and piecing together, there's little rehashing and reheating. It's kind of beautiful.)

While working on his research paper the young man of the present managed to obtain documents detailing the case against the arrested and subsequently executed parents of the young man of the past. Participants in the Memorial competition are encouraged to turn to eyewitnesses when they can be found and to archives where they're accessible. The young man did all that and was diligently going through the documents when he noticed the name of the officer who interrogated the parents.

Irina Sherbakova is telling this story to Natella Boltyanskaya in an interview on Echo of Moscow radio station (still independent, still going strong). It is at this point in her story that the historian pauses long enough for the journalist to exhale 'oh god' anticipating the next turn, hoping—you can hear it in her exhalation—that she is wrong. But no, Natella Boltyanskaya is right, it's just as she thought: the interrogating officer and the young man of the present have the same surname. In small towns, the kind the two young men come from, certain surnames are claimed by families and clans, not by page after page of phonebooks. And now the young man of the present is beginning to unravel. Perhaps before he got hold of this diary and followed the young man of the past through the shock and shame of his grief and ostracism, the young man of the present would have been not nearly so devastated by the possibility of his grandfather working for the NKVD, but the young man of the past has done his work and now it matters enormously to the young man of the present which side of the interrogating table his grandfather once sat on. In imagining what his grandfather did and did not do, the young man of the present has to withstand a double blow (or, more precisely, suffer a double wound)—to himself as the inheritor of his family's history, and to the young man of the past who has become like a ghostly brother to him.

The young man of the present did not set out to dig up his family's history. Suspecting nothing, he was on no mission to get to some buried truth. He was ambushed. He was tripped up. The past found him. It grabbed him through a complete stranger's story and spun him into the vortex of his own family's history. So much of the past works like that. It's vortex-like. Doesn't live in little zoo enclosures. Cannot be visited like an ageing aunt. It's engine-like. At least in certain places it is like a criminal's mark burned into your family's skin (I got this image from the accidentally revealed fleur-de-lis on Milady's shoulder in Dumas's *Three Musketeers*). 'The past shapes the present'— they teach people that in schools and universities. *Shapes?* Infiltrates more like, imbues, infuses, it is invisible this past, it is gas not solid, an odourless, colourless chemical agent bouncing around in the lungs, crackling in the spaces between us, in the air the culture breathes in, out.

It transpired that the identical surname was a coincidence. But no relief flowed for the young man of the present. His grandfather, says Irina Sherbakova, turned out to be a much more monstrous man than the provincial interrogator his grandson briefly imagined him to be. 'Oh no, oh god'... I swear I can hear it in Natella Boltyanskaya's voice—*this will never end, this will go on forever*. 'But we should not be afraid of this stuff, we should not be afraid of the psychological shock suffered by this young man,' says Sherbakova.

Be afraid of its opposite—of the absence of shocks. Of bumping into no diaries and being waylaid by no surnames.

GIVE ME A CHILD BEFORE
THE AGE OF SEVEN AND I WILL
SHOW YOU THE WOMAN

PRE

Once I was a young woman. Dyed my dark hair blonde and accidentally made it orange. We'd have been in Australia two years max. Put some grey dye on top of the orange to tame the orange. Still pretty bad but OK enough to leave the house. My dark roots started growing straight away. My eyebrows were dark. Men liked it. I got myself—don't ask me how—into a broadcast journalism course. It was for Australia's non-native sons and daughters—this is how—and there I met Nahji. Nahji Chu who would become misschu, trailblazing this and groundbreaking that, businesswoman of the year, food-fashion icon and then, mere minutes later, woman on the tip of losing it all rescued at the eleventh hour by the same guy, we're told, who pulled Bevilles the jeweller and biscuit maker Unibic out of the abyss.

It is not like the story will end here either.

The journalism course where Nahji and I met was before all that. I liked her. She liked me. I was lying about my age (seventeen, pretending to be twenty-four). She had plenty of things she wasn't telling, not about her age though, age wasn't a problem. She was twenty, twenty-one, one of six, somewhere in the middle, the oldest daughter. Her family was Vietnamese. Escaping Laos by boat they'd got caught and spent three years in Thai refugee camps. She was nine when they reached Australia. At a dinner at my parents' place (we didn't do dinner *parties*) Nahji said all her family's money was sewn inside a belt. We loved her unwishywashiness, how whole she felt.

Next time I saw her was on *Q&A* on TV. How many years later? I am counting. Possibly even twenty. She was nearly the same, so assured, emitting power. Sheer voltage, that was the difference. No one is the same after twenty years. And a year or so after that, things were still on the up for her then, we met in Sydney where she lived 'on the edges of Kings Cross' (made me laugh) as one newspaper phrased it in her apartment I'd already seen photos of on websites, in fashion pages—yeah, it looked that good to me too except what you did not get from the photographs was a feeling of her standing apart from everyone else. Alone. Or maybe I got it wrong and that was just me coming at her from some pre-misschu past and making her remember something, the time, its passing, I felt it too. Her bulldog George—he got mentioned in almost every write-up—barked, jumped, ate sausage with conviction, peed outside. There we were. I liked her. She liked me.

After a while you start noticing how much of their childhood is in people around you. In your twenties, thirties, teens definitely, the childhood stuff often feels like a cliché. Doesn't seem the force it will show itself to be later. Even recently, I hear Ira Glass from *This American Life* radio show say there's 'always a story from childhood we have at the ready to explain to others who we are' and I think how in America, America in particular, childhood has for so long been used as self-explanation, or some form of self-diagnosis, and how regularly this verges on a cop-out, personally, culturally, also how blinding such determinism can be, flattening too, like a life's a by-the-numbers backstory in an undistinguished Hollywood movie. Yet I see as well—took me a while—that of a million things happening to us in babydom, toddlerhood, prepubescence, some are bound to turn into what Eva Hoffman calls 'needles'. Needles that 'pricked your flesh' then 'could never be extracted again'.

I was standing in Nahji's apartment, Nahji who in a short span of fame had put a thousand and one misschu quotes and quotelets out there but couldn't be made fully bland even by the journos paid to dutifully banalify her. You still got a sense of her: an arrow midflight, deep inside her own trajectory, forensic about Point B. Nearly all the profiles retraced her route. From poverty-blasted refugee to multimillion-dollar entrepreneur, from escaping her past to embracing it, from shame to pride in her identity, from nothing to a something that felt nearly like everything—and the media especially dug the misfires. How she tried to sew, make films, act, go corporate, and when all the above got her nowhere *Chu decided the only way forward was to play the cards she'd been dealt.* The cards were these: Vietnamese, food, hard work, ingenuity, don't expect anyone to give you anything, lucky to end up in Australia where most people are asleep at the wheel.

Something bothered me, and it wasn't the underplaying of the sheer wildness of her detours. Nahji had done so many things before misschu our journalism course did not get a mention. It was that the whole Cinderella Chu scenario allowed no glimpse of what she was actually up against. For instance: the world would be a different place if every seventeenth refugee with an alpha personality and a stomach for work could dream and build something deemed of lasting value. Easier instead for a camel to go through the eye of a needle. The probability of Nahji attempting the peculiar thing that is misschu and succeeding in even an up, down, rich-then-not sort of way has always been minuscule. She borrowed zero money to get started or keep going ('people in finance would forever put me down and say I should borrow'), didn't have a marketing team, let her gut decide prices ('I don't need to weigh ingredients to work out what to charge'), undertook no market research, commissioned high-end experimental art projects, stuck to the same menu. Same menu why? 'Easy to change a menu,' she tells me, 'hardest is to cook the same thing day in and out.'

She said to her staff, 'Imagine cooking the same dish all your life to perfection. That's what I ask you to do. You should be able to meditate through work. Unless you can do that, you shouldn't be working here.'

Would you have your balls, Nahji, I ask her, if you did not have to grow them in refugee camps of Thailand and then in Australia, the coveted, plentiful Australia, which proved more of a camp than the actual camps? Would you have your commander-in-chief streak if you did not empirically discover early you could make your older siblings follow you, and other kids of varying ages and abilities followed you too, and you could lead your little armies and quench their little mutinies and give life to ideas that come specifically into your and no one else's head? And you could do these things anywhere.

The boat, belt, camp, no money, plenty of shame—they're what shows up on the X-ray scan, right?

Nahji has an unmuddled way of speaking. Gaps between her words are unsmudged even when she's hesitating, or debating with herself. 'Look at the six of us, in my family, we are all close in age, all thinking differently, living different lives. How many people come from war zones, from broken history, a broken family? Not everyone becomes an entrepreneur, not everyone is driven. If we were all sum totals of our histories there'd be a lot more competition for someone like me.'

A certain kind of strength is innate not learned she says. It's an individual thing. You find it and you hone it. You draw on the past too but the thing is there at the start, a birthmark. Then she says, 'The refugee thing is not what drives me. When we arrived in Australia we were like the last rung in the society, like rejects, I was ashamed of being Vietnamese then. At my first primary school my only friend was an Aboriginal girl. We were two people no one spoke to, no one wanted to touch. This sticks in my mind more than the refugee camps.'

The camps were harsh but made OK by the resourcefulness of Vietnamese families in them. 'If you put us in a jail,' is how Nahji explains it, 'we'd probably make a school out of it, and we did, we formed clusters of schools in a refugee camp. We taught ourselves. We grew veggies. Made things out of clay. Made a clay oven. Made fire. We knitted.' Nahji came up with an idea for a theatre company, staging shadow-puppet performances behind a bedsheet using a torch and handmade clay characters. She'd stand at the door collecting money—nothing good in life is free. If the kids had no coins she accepted scarab beetles, seeds, matchsticks, something exotic, anything of value. No one was turned back. She was wanting an audience. But she also wanted this to be a proper exchange. It upsets her, the way people in today's refugee camps are pressed into involuntary, demeaning idleness, at least this is what's shown in the media—you don't see people making things. Having no way of passing skills or knowledge, no meaningful exchanges of goods and services, destroys people, that's what she thinks.

The belief that we may look at children at certain points in their life and predict something of the adults they will become has been around since childhood came to be reckoned a distinct phase in a human life. The modern-day pop version goes we can glimpse, or see squarely, the future grown-up in a seven-year-old Jenna or Timothy. Easygoing Timothy will sail into well-adjusted adulthood barring cataclysms while little spoilt princess Jenna will stomp through life expecting people to accommodate her view of the world until she may, or may not, run into enough brick walls to concuss the sense of entitlement out of her. Or: Jenna who cries when shown a picture of a wounded doggie will grow up to be a social worker, Timothy whose eyes stay dry as dust will wind up a lawyer specialising in corporate takeovers.

Nahji at seven? Freezeframe her, cute and bossy, in a refugee camp, what do you get? She could grow up to be a junkie or philanthropist. Or artist, businesswoman of the decade, abject failure, inspiration, a conqueror, the conquered, mother of many, mother of none, down and out in the suburbs, opening a flagship tuckshop in London (it'll go bust and the four Sydney ones will get sold off but that is so not the point). Nahji is marked by her early history, that's for certain, yet she could go this way or that. Or *first* this way *then* that. She is as elusive as Douglas Fairbanks's bemasked Zorro.

Everywhere is Nahji's refugee visa. On menus, delivery

bike baskets, napkin dispensers, tuckshop walls—along with her siblings' visas it is the centrepiece of misschu design. She says it's a beautiful image. Arresting, and it tells a story, tells you why it's called misschu, makes people realise it's a surname and a play on words. 'It's retaliation too.' 'For what?' I ask. Not needing to ask. 'For racism. For being ashamed of who I was.' I wonder if she was worried it'd seem kitsch. 'No, I was worried about my family's response and whether it was legal to display the documents.' It's retaliation and it's marketing. Her slow-drip style. Those people entering her tuckshops not on the back of media hoo-ha but who stumble in because of the look or smell or location will order, eat, pore over their phones, notice something out the corner of one eye, go home. Good. Then on their third or, let's say, fourth visit they may peer closer at the walls or menu logo and then it's 'oh, I didn't realise' and they may see the stamps and the dates and ask the staff what's going on here and the staff will give them the short or long answer and they might go home and google and discover more. That's how she likes it. Getting under customers' skins. Getting them to wonder. Then ... a gradual revelation. She likes it when staff tell her she made who they are cool. They're proud working for her, it seems, no matter the fierce temper, the dogs unleashed by her perfectionism.

In interviews Nahji says Vietnamese is not simply a food option that's cheap; it's food with a profound history. 'Love my food, you've also got to love my culture.' At first I think the refugee design elements are in poor taste. Interesting idea but come on. Desperation, pain, shame, fear, bodies buried in oceans or unmarked graves in other people's countries—these are your *branding apparatus*? To one interviewer she says, 'Placing a complex identity, one that has survived trauma and racism, at the forefront of a commercial venture is unusual.' Yep. But I see it. She is interested in generating power before empathy, and talking's for later. 'People don't listen to stories unless they can eat them or feel them or wear them,' she tells me.

That time in her apartment, I'd said—I was remembering her at my parents' house, how solid she seemed to us, how at ease in this world that clearly was not hers—'After everything does Australia feel like something approximating home?'

'No. I don't think anywhere is going to feel like home for me. I don't want anywhere to feel like home. I don't want to anchor like that.'

'You don't ache for a sense of home?'

'I want to have a big yacht. Why? Because I don't think I will ever be truly welcomed anywhere. In Sydney they remind you that you are not from here. I beat them to it. I say "you ling, we bling" so you cannot say it to me. I make fun of myself before you can make fun of me. And I say this is not my home. Before you can say it, I've already announced it.'

You ling, we bling—misschu's home delivery slogan. 'The best defence is attack.' Who said that? I grew up with this saying so it feels kind of self-evidently true. Here we go again. *Grew up with it.*

'I rarely read,' Nahji says. 'I can count the number of books I have read on one hand.' It's a warning not confession. She knows I read and I write and this stuff must matter to me, and that my assessment of people probably takes in their need for books and that the world outside, too, likes to think people like her rose from their refugee camps and smelly first kitchens to the top of the charts not merely by working seven days a week and never having holidays but by being smart about it. Not just breaking their backs and ripping their arseholes like their parents and their parents' parents. Sucking the knowledge in. Riding it, like the big blue whale. Nahji's talent is not in synthesising and building on whatever is out there already. It's conjuring what is not there. 'There are no magazines on my table,' she says to me. 'I hate them. And I am afraid of them. I don't look at magazines because I am scared if I come up with an idea, it's someone else's. I come up with my own ideas. If it happens to be the same as someone else's at least I came up with it.'

Way back before her London tuckshop went kaput and Nahji faced losing the lot, I was walking through the Melbourne Now exhibition at the National Gallery of Victoria and saw a Lucy McRae short film commissioned by Nahji with misschu imprints all over it. Nahji had sent me a disk sometime earlier and I'd watched it on a computer but here it occupied a wall. It was looping away, as if it were an art object like any other. I sat and watched it roll through then start again. Cloning, the edible self, a blurring of the boundaries between body and food, between what is now and what's to come. Would you believe Nahji sneaked an ad for her business into the National Gallery of Vic?

• • •

It's said Jesuits first said 'give me a child before the age of seven and I'll show you the man' and this, as things Jesuit tend to, carries queasy-making undertones of an institution sucking up a child and spewing up a complete, morally delineated being.

Education, indoctrination, values inculcation, etc.—that's a caricature mostly, an unthinking bit of Jesuit-creaming, besides writer Barry Lopez said it was his Jesuit teachers who woke in him a 'capacity for metaphor', also it appears the axiom may have been widely misinterpreted anyway. Never mind. I intend leaving Jesuits in peace. Growing up in the Soviet Union, seven as a cut-off age felt natural despite my peers and me never having heard of Jesuits and their axioms in our atheist paradise. Seven, or just before seven, was when you went to school. So a period of childhood in which your family could have greater influence than state institutions over your life ended, unless you were outlandishly lucky. We pre-institutionalised (correction: pre-overinstitutionalised) seven-year-olds, children of *dvory* and empty flats, were carriers of a foundational self, which was our own homespun mutation of let's call it crudely (because we can) the Jesuit axiom. Still, the seven bit stuck.

Hanging low and loose in the air like an unmanned hot-air blimp all my life has been the axiom's god-free version—whatever can be non-genetically encoded in a human being is encoded before birth and then before the age of seven. Encoded mightn't be the best word, and the computer metaphors sitting as they do on the tips of our tongues, hardwired, hardware, software, may not be right either. Perhaps saying something is constructed before the age of seven, an armature, a casing, a slab of circuitry, a monopile, gets us closer to the essence of the idea (the idea that is also very much a feeling). Something is constructed that is hard to get at and dismantle or overwrite afterwards.

Scientists and theologians like to reach for a tree. All parts of a tree above ground are dependent on sun, rain, wind, oxygen, birds, neighbourhood kids, roaming catclaw. Whereas a tree's roots are underground and invisible unless the tree is in trouble or dead. The root system is our early childhood. Not only the roots, the soil around them, also worm armies, subterranean bodies of water. The roots' functions are obvious, to provide essential food and drink not obtainable elsewhere to the tree, and they are the tree's foundation.

Tree may be the most hardworking metaphor in the world. A supreme metaphor is also a supreme artifice. Tree roots that grow on the surface, or in water, under pavement, inside shopping centres as is often seen, are not part of this picture because there is something about those archetypal roots in the ground—the way they are both secretive and sustaining, buried deep yet at the centre of things, resistant to change and protected against change. It fits. Fits our idea of the beginnings of selfhood. And when people talk of 'rediscovering our roots' they are talking about, beyond the wish to reconnect with the world of their parents, rediscovering the cultural and sensory environment that, in concert with genes and whatever else, produced their early selves. They are talking about following landing lights to something we might call our nature, which, as Heraclitus told us back in BC, *hides from us but wants to be found*.

Nature, nurture—this thing cannot be worked out, as they used to say in my childhood, without half a litre of vodka. My erudite former dentist told me recently about going on a study tour to China in the 1980s with a group of fellow Australian dentists. Walking through a teaching hospital full of people stricken with illnesses the Australians had only previously seen in textbooks, they came by a large hall. Inside the hall fifty or more dentists were treating without a drop of anaesthetic young children, as was the norm then in the non-West. This hall was an open-plan, teeth-drilling quarry. And, my ex-dentist said, 'you could hear a pin drop. It's the culture of not showing pain and each of these kids was totally schooled in it already.'

Almost two decades before that conversation I had a conversation with a friend whose parents divorced when she was young. My friend believed I was OK, positively blasé at times, about raising a child on my own because my parents stayed together and I hadn't experienced a 'broken' home and thus didn't have inside of me her gut-dread of replicating it for my children. I did not buy my friend's theory. No way was I some product of a lack of family dysfunction. Simply, I wanted children and abhorred domesticity as I understood it then—an image in my head of me holding hands in a suburban supermarket with the father of a child I had recently borne felt like capitulation without grace. After a while I stopped thinking my friend was merely talking to herself. To be alive for X number of years is to know people have children in all permutations possible for every reason under the sun. For most the past is only one persistent voice in the ear, often monosyllabic, yes, no, no, yes. And when in my early twenties I was alone with that child of mine and no sirens were howling, icy winds did not tear through me, gates weren't shutting automatically, doors weren't locking themselves, it's clear—clear *now*—I was free of any subcellular struggle between my family's past and the future I was imagining, piece by piece, for myself, so yeah I see my friend was (50%) right.

Nurture, nature—in ways too complex to lead to scientific or cultural consensus they are in it together, and each word may mean a thousand things. Bubbling in the witches' brew aren't only genes and environment. There's prenatal, perinatal experience. And something called our prenatal personality; and (what else?) chance. The child, the human coming out of the pot is herself, as research on neuroplasticity and the changing brain tells us, a work in progress.

Psychologist Stuart Derbyshire at the University of Birmingham calls the idea of a person's early years deciding their fate a 'pseudo-science of the parent bashers'. Psychologist Oliver James thinks the notion parental influence may be unimportant to a person's development is 'garbage, postmodern drivel'. Cognitive psychologist and linguist Steven Pinker says 'to acknowledge human nature, many think, is to endorse racism, sexism, war, greed, genocide, nihilism, reactionary politics, and neglect of children and the disadvantaged'. Physician-philosopher Raymond Tallis writes 'if you come across a new discipline with the prefix "neuro" and it is not to do with the nervous system, switch on your bullshit detector. If it has society in its sights, reach for your gun.'

We're past newborn-as-a-blank-slate, past the thick bushes of social Darwinism, past behaviourism and genetic supremacism. But we are in another thick forest. Trees again. Maybe it's for the best. Worst would be to convince ourselves we know.

After Andrew Solomon spent time with Sue and Tom Klebold, parents of Dylan Klebold, who together with a friend killed twelve students and one teacher at Columbine High School in Colorado before turning their guns on themselves and who had bombs planted too, which didn't go off, Solomon described the parents as 'victims of the terrifying, profound unknowability of even the most intimate human relationship'.

With killers it's human habit to think back to their family

and childhood. Genghis Khan was beaten and abused as a boy, my erudite current dentist mentioned just the other day. Anders Breivik's childhood and psychosexually warped relationship with his mum is central to the way him becoming a mass murderer of Norway's young people gets told and understood. Solomon could find nothing in the Klebold family's home life. No abuse, neglect, detachment. Instead: love, acceptance, kindness, warmth.

What happens to nature v. nurture when the person, one's intimate, is potentially unknowable? Or maybe the point is we know quite a lot but this knowledge cannot be settled into a pattern, smoothed out. It must remain tense with contradictions and limit cases, must sit uncomfortably within us like a provisional government at a rushed dawn assembly.

• • •

When Rhea Dempsey was doing workshop after workshop she could walk into a roomful of pregnant women and see—it's as if she was wearing special glasses—the imprints of their own birth on the women in front of her. Not just their birth, she tells me, but their first months in the world. It was like the moment after the Big Bang when both matter and antimatter rush apart filling the universe, and there it was caught in the faces of women turned towards her.

Rhea's been at it close to forty years—more than a thousand births (one was my dark-eyed son) as a birth attendant. She has steered through labour women who once fell out of their mothers' bodies into her arms. When Rhea's own three girls were young they went to a small community-run primary school where Rhea taught swimming. She'd been at the birth of at least half those kids and could see their births in how they swam. 'You could pick,' she says, 'the kids who rushed out of their mothers' bodies and the ones who had a long, slow birth.' One boy in swimming class whose birth Rhea was at had an 'uncomfortable position in his mother's womb, all skewed, twisted' and he could not swim in a straight line.

Rhea tells parents to watch their kids early, before the world gets in there and starts hammering at them—watch how they crawl. The way they begin to walk. Watch closely. She says these things are 'a pure expression of who that child is'. Also children will never change as much as they do in the first year of their lives. 'It sets up our yearly rhythm and a sort of template.'

'Who the child is' is Rhea's big question.

(Who are the children before they become who we think they are? Before they become who they think they are?)

'My biggest passion,' Rhea says, 'is allowing children the clearest form of entry into the world.'

Years ago at a talk on pain in labour I was sitting waiting for it to start—thirty-two weeks pregnant with my second child and thinking I don't need anyone special with me when I'm giving birth not because I was arrogant or spoilt by an easy labour the first time around but because I thought, apart from midwives doing what they do, and your family doing what it does, nothing else really needs doing. In walked Rhea. She was dressed in white. I remember the jolt of her white—it was as if someone rode a camel into that chewed-up room leased from a high school—and I remember too what Rhea wore when she came to the Royal Women's Hospital where I was losing my mind already in a ward so featureless it reappears to me now simply as a dimly lit rectangle. Leather gloves, sharp boots and a shawl draped over her back. I was naked. I didn't know anymore what my body was doing. And everything on her was beautiful and extra-crunchy clean as if she made a point of not protecting her nice clothes from me.

After the pain talk I'd gone up to her. 'I know it's too late and you are all booked up and whatever,' I said, 'but will you please be with me during labour because I didn't know till now how much I need you there?'

And she said 'yes' and she said 'OK'. I'd forgotten what it was like to need help from a stranger. And to ask for it? I doubt I had ever known how.

Rhea in a room of women... I like to imagine her looking. I don't mind if I am one of the women. I am not precious. I want Rhea to read me. A while back I watched, compulsively even, Tim Roth in that slimy TV outing *Lie to Me* and learned that forty-three muscles combine to produce ten thousand possible facial expressions and when people lie they look—though it'd take a face reader to notice it—left or right or down or up, one of these four, correct me if I'm wrong, all bullshit no doubt except, when it's not, it can be awe-making. The noticing. How some people are preternaturally good at it. Nothing escapes their eyes it seems. To be seen right through by that one person—is this not one of the great, unspoken human needs?

What I am actually wondering is whether there could be a mark on us, an original barcode, a document not of a life lived but of our beginnings, of a self on the cusp of history, and whether this barcode might be visible to one, two people in the whole world—people who have seen enough human nakedness perhaps, enough onions unpeeling themselves, to know what's in front of them?

Not 0 to 7 then but 0 to 0.

V.W.

Patient goes to doctor. 'Doctor,' he says, 'you have to help me, I am in desperate need. I'm pissing everywhere.' Doctor gives him a tablet and tells him to come back. In a few days as agreed the patient comes back. 'Hello doctor, how are you, how is your wife?' the patient says cheerfully. 'What a positively lovely day it is.' The doctor is bemused and asks: 'And how is your condition?' 'Oh, it's great, doctor. I'm pissing everywhere but I don't give a fuck about it anymore.'

Roman Polanski told this joke to Vera Wasowski sometime in the 1960s when they saw each other in London. Polanski lived in London then, post-Poland, pre-Hollywood. He took Vera to some fancy club frequented, so he mentioned in passing, by Mick Jagger. She remembers the joke but forgets the club's name. It was the Ad Lib club—see a 1983 Clive James interview with Polanski, post-Hollywood by then. Vera in the 1960s was living in Australia, dreamy dull flatland which was nothing much like London of the 1960s, not at all like Warsaw of the 1950s—what are the stats? Gone, 85 to 90% of it, in the war. The 'most agonising spot in the whole of terrorised

Europe' said poet Czeslaw Milosz yet a city which allowed the flourishing, only a few years later, of people Vera calls, insistently, 'intellectual elites'. She says 'top'. She says 'world class'.

They'd all come together, filmmakers, journalists, actors, intellectuals, Andrzej Wajda in whose *Pokolenie* Polanski made his acting debut, Vera, her journalist-husband Jan; they would get in one room. And sparks! Wasn't the doctor-patient joke actually about them? The ability to not give a fuck—was it not one of the few freedoms possible in their country now it had been Stalinised? Whatever was being surrendered and taken over in the outside world, the inside of one's head was one potentially unreachable place. Most of the people around Vera and Jan in Warsaw in the 1950s had that place inside that belonged to them only. The state's fingerprints were all over work you did, streets you walked, the whole school-university-job-pension track. You had to register your typewriters. The air itself was like that: breathe in and out, once, and you were implicated. But there were ways of being free or at least acting as if you were free, ways of blending with no wallpaper. Watch Vera and Jan and you'd know. It was possible to cultivate a willed conspicuousness. To banish meekness. And channel abandonment. Let's say you were not circumspect about the volume at which you spoke in public and not fastidiously self-censoring about the contents of your speech either, and your quantities of alcohol drunk weren't moderate and you were, maybe, borderline scandalous in how you did love, sex, family while the poems you'd memorised were poems of Adam Mickiewicz, who considered Poland the Christ of nations, not those by some servility-extolling, drum-beating Party stooge.

Poetry, art, drinking, affairs. These were not luxuries or

sweeteners, no. Not extra-political digressions. It was all too easy to rage deep inside at a regime that, as poet Adam Zagajewski wrote, had no time for agriculture or architecture or literature or the railway system but time without limit for its army, police, speeches, parades. The trick said Zagajewski was 'to conquer totalitarianism in passing, on our way to greater things'. Lest you become defined by your opposition to it. Lest you get enslaved by the fight against it. So many surrounding you did. One of the twentieth century's lessons went precisely: sooner or later you become what you fight. So: poetry, art, drinking, affairs… Essential inoculations?

No. Yes. What they did was produce a wildness, a state of constant incalculable movement of the soul. As long as the soul kept moving, expanding, opening its chambers, speeding up and slowing down like a wise fugitive who knows how to run in large open spaces while evading a sniper lying in wait, it could not be co-opted fully. Were these inoculations enough? Yes. No. To most questions about Poland lurk two answers minimum. In Milosz's book *The Captive Mind* is a version, more an inversion, of Polanski's doctor joke. The 'Pill of Murti-Bing', a fictional wonderdrug Milosz encountered in a little-known 1927 Polish novel by Stanislaw Ignacy Witkiewicz, soothes nagging dread, making those who pop it 'impervious to any metaphysical concerns' and, soon enough, welcoming of imminent invader dictatorships from the East. Witkiewicz killed himself on 18th September 1939 after learning the Red Army had crossed Poland's eastern border. Milosz defected to the West in 1951 after spending the entire five years of German occupation in Warsaw. Perhaps the doubleness of the doctor joke was always there. Perhaps the doubleness of the joke was the joke.

When Poland was overrun Polanski was six. Vera—a year younger. Out of a million Polish Jewish children younger than fourteen about five thousand were alive by war's end. Most survived the way Polanski and Vera survived, hiding in convents, boarding schools, orphanages, on farms, in attics, with Christian families. In holes, caves, forests, between false walls, in cupboards. Jan's survival was different; he was in Kazakhstan. Jan's father, editor of a Jewish newspaper when Jewish newspapers still existed in Poland, had the foresight to get his family out. At their second romantic dinner Vera told Jan about what happened to her. She was brief, rolled the whole thing into a few sentences, no drawn-out sagas. He, her formidable future husband, could not drive back tears.

Vera and Jan stayed in Warsaw until the late 1950s. They were happy, on fire, in a bubble of their own. It's rare you hear of people having the time of their lives in postwar Poland, Jews no less. Bigmouthed, bigheaded, visible-from-outer-space Jews. Everyone knows when the war ended virtually no Jews were left in Warsaw—same Warsaw that before 1939 had the second-largest Jewish community after New York—but Vera and Jan were still there, Polanski was there. There were, Vera says, plenty of Jews among their friends. Many, like Vera, were not Warsawians to start with. Most belonged to a special category best described by poet Aleksander Wat. (Try speaking about Poland without turning to its poets. Impossible: perhaps it's because as philosopher Agamben wrote in *Remnants of Auschwitz* 'the "witness" gesture is also that of the poet'.) Wat, when asked whether he was Polish or Jewish, replied 'I'm Polish-Polish and Jewish-Jewish.' You were not one or the other, you were both at twice the intensity. Some of the most prominent professors at Warsaw University where Vera studied journalism, a degree she regarded as brilliant not least because of the quality of the teaching faculty and breadth of its intellectual concerns, were Jewish too, and most of them, these last professors standing, would be expelled from their positions in the late 1960s when Władysław Gomułka's 'anti-Zionist' campaign took care of the remnants of the city's Jewish intelligentsia. Vera and Jan considered leaving only when they glimpsed, as she puts it, 'anti-Semitism go bananas'. It had never gone away, that indestructible Polish anti-Semitism. It was there waiting bitter, capable of murder, for survivors straight after the war. Come 1956—Gomułka's burst of de-Stalinisation—it soared like a long-winged bird.

One night in 1956 they were all sitting in a nightclub. 'A very high-profile group,' Vera says, 'of friends. The top intellectual group.' Fifty-six: time of a peculiarly semi-totalitarian government that 'allowed one to think but not to speak, allowed one to hum but forbade singing, allowed one to rest but didn't allow one to work, allowed one to enter a church but would not consent to have one leave it'—Zagajewski, with his glorious precision. Strange, strange times and at some point the nightclub conversation took a turn and they were talking about the next Holocaust in Poland. Was it, in fact, beyond contemplation? And one man in their group, a famous actor, non-Jewish, dead now, got on his knees, in jest, or maybe in a moment of intense actorly sincerity, and declared facing Vera—she was, you can safely assume, the most dazzling woman in that club— 'I would hide you. Don't worry.'

This did it for her. How could anyone entertain on any level the possibility of another Holocaust? In Poland of all places, so soon after. Hiding her, oh you great, fearless benefactor—she felt sick.

Nathan Englander has a story called 'What We Talk About When We Talk About Anne Frank', a reworking of Raymond Carver's 'What We Talk About When We Talk About Love'. Englander's story is about the first afternoon together in god knows how long for two middle-aged Jewish couples. The wives, Debbie and Lauren, used to be best friends at their orthodox all-girls school in New York. Then they got married. Deb stayed in the States, turned secular, had a son, bought a house with a pool; Lauren ran to Israel, turned Hasidic, had ten daughters, she's Shoshana not Lauren now. The couples meet in the south Florida house of the couple who stayed put. They talk, drink vodka, smoke the dope Deb's son hid in the laundry, search the pantry for kosher food (munchies) after some 'mixed dancing' in the rain and it is all painfully tense, especially between the husbands, and, more than once, it is painfully beautiful too.

That pantry and the bathroom next to it are designed in such a way they can be sealed from the rest of the house. Put a wall up and no one would ever know. Deb whose grandparents were born in the Bronx (someone please calculate how many miles from Europe) made it so, and the pantry is stacked with food and Deb likes to play a game, a serious thought experiment she says, an active pathology thinks her husband who nonetheless plays along this time, called the Anne Frank game. Otherwise known as the Who Will Hide Me? game or the Righteous Gentile game. Self-explanatory. And Lauren takes it on and after a while she says, you know, you can play it against yourselves too—if one of you wasn't Jewish, would you hide the other? And at first it seems nonsensical but then they do try that one on. Then they do.

In Carver's story, the couples drink and they talk about love and when they finish they've talked themselves into some new and frightening world order. (The last passage gives a clue: 'I could hear my heart beating. I could hear everyone's heart. I could hear the human noise we sat there making, not one of us moving, not even when the room went dark.') In Englander's story too the two couples cannot move by the end. They've unleashed something and who knows if they can walk back from it. Or back to *where*? Critics—some, not all—have written an American Holocaust is so insane Englander's game is meaningless. Worse: it's unforgivably relativist, insultingly moralising. Surely though to live in the shadow of the great holocausts of the twentieth century is to live with these questions. And surely the Anne Frank game is only as obscene in America or Australia, now, as in the 1950s in Poland where Vera had to face the actor on his expressive knees. It—and the Plantation Owner game? the Slave Merchant game? the NKVD game?— has to be obscene wherever you play it, because to contemplate people being forced again into those choices is intolerable, and because talking about it if you didn't live it and not talking about it—as if it could never happen to you and yours, as if anyone could ever be immune or exempt, as if *you would know* what to do if it came to your door—are as obscene as each other.

Eva S, born in Bratislava, is speaking fifty years after the war in Paul Valent's book *Child Survivors of the Holocaust*: 'Whenever I come into a room, I feel I have to decide who is to live. Even at the dinner table with my children, I think "my God, whom would I choose if I had to?"' Eva S was at Auschwitz with her younger sister Marta. Both Eva and Marta were selected for his experiments by Dr Mengele. Mengele made children play a Farmer Wants a Wife game in which they believed they were picking a child who would go on to die. Valent describes Mengele's game as the ultimate in evil. Vera was spared having to choose but, as a child, saw others' soul-eviscerating choices. Or perhaps survivors are never spared. Perhaps the knowledge of the choices is always with them and it leads them through life, this knowledge, like an Ariadne's thread.

In a different lifetime after Jan's death from chronic alcoholism in Australia, Vera will seriously consider going back to Poland. She will say to herself, 'What the fuck am I doing in Australia?' A friend, the head of a TV station in Warsaw, promises her a job pretty much on arrival. She goes for a visit. And one day walking someplace in the centre of Warsaw, people everywhere, sun shining, she will see on a wall JUDEN RAUS all freshly sprayed and glistening in its newness. And she will know what maybe she had always known— no coming back.

Eva Hoffman, born in Poland two months after the war to Holocaust survivor parents, speaks of 'a head-on clash of two martyrological memories' of the war on Polish soil—clash of the Polish, the Jewish. To both, the 'desperate defensiveness and bitterness of the mutual accusations … appear … as a mockery of their own tragedy, and a travesty of their moral truth'.

In Australia, to which he never reconciled himself, Jan would remember the people around them in Warsaw—their circle—and lament Vera's willingness to 'lower her intellectual standards'. He never 'lowered' his. What to do with the unfairness of it all? She did not want to come to Australia. It was Israel she was pining for after the war when Israel was not even Israel yet. She pined for it again in the 1950s. First time her mother stopped her; the second time, Jan. 'I am not going to replace one totalitarian country with another,' he said. This is how they—Vera, Jan, Vera's son from her first marriage, Vera's mother—ended up in Australia. That Jan didn't 'lower his standards' would in time become a familiar tragedy of the intellectual in exile never quite making peace with the new country. She made it of course. She would have made it on Mars in a paper bag like Matt Damon in that movie *The Martian*. What was being in Australia compared to the childhood she had? Vera made it and she stayed true to the Vera she became in Warsaw. How many can say that?

• • •

First Vera and I went to her old butcher around the corner from Acland Street.

—Hello. Good to see you again. How are you?

—I'm still alive, as you see. Still walking.

—I'm still alive too.

(A conversation not at all morbid, almost joyful.)

Then we went to Woolworths for some anti-cold medicine and thick toilet paper—the friend she was staying with in St Kilda had toilet paper you could put your finger through. Then we walked to a Jewish deli on Balaclava Road. Vera wanted chopped liver. I knew the deli owner; our daughters had played together in sunny pre-hormonal days. I hugged the owner. 'She comes here all the time,' the owner said to me in Russian, looking at Vera. Then: 'She is a good woman.' I was pretty sure Vera could understand what we were saying but I still replied in Russian, 'She has quite a story on her.' 'Yes, well, all my clients have a story on them,' the owner said. 'The ones with tattooed numbers have pretty much died out but the ones who still come have a story and a half too.' This was, I noted to myself, the best conversation the deli owner and I had had to date.

In another shop—what were we buying? something small and edible I think—the man behind the counter wanted to know if we were related, which counts as small talk these days, one step up from topsy-turvy weather. 'We are friends,' I said, hoping it was not too ostentatious to claim something we hadn't grown into yet. 'She is my granddaughter,' said Vera.

Shopping with Vera: the wildness, bigness of her bursting out in the most banal, microscopic exchanges like a button on a blouse popping and underneath is a patch of skin that speaks of another, unfathomable life.

I am writing about Vera because she is unlike all the other child Holocaust survivors I've met or read about. She drinks, smokes, parties, drops names. Always has. She is prickly. She's had lots of men. The word people routinely use for her is 'outrageous'. Other survivors tend to keep their distance from Vera. Yet she has oodles of people in her orbit. Her distaste for petty bourgeoisie—another defining characteristic—is almost Flaubertian. Flaubert who once signed a note to his friend Louis Bouilhet: *Gustavus Flaubertus, Bourgeoisophobus*. Easy to imagine in big letters

VERA WASOWSKI.

BOURGEOISOPHOBUS.

On the March of the Living, a three-kilometre walk from

Auschwitz to Birkenau, she managed to piss off a lot of the Australian contingent not only with her refusals to behave herself but with her frequently declared love of Polish food and countryside. Loving Poland, no matter how complicated and contradictory that love, no matter that Vera was expressing her love in a new century, remains taboo for many survivors and their families. 'Vera's view of the world,' one of the March of the Living organisers told me, 'was antithetical to most in the group.' These were conservative middle-class people reconnecting with their family histories. Vera: an alien in their midst. Organisers: frustrated? Yes, definitely frustrated by the end and wanting to know why on this earth of all earths she came on the trip. 'I am here because of the anti-Semitism in Poland,' Vera told them, 'I want to make a stand.'

I first see Vera's name in a soupy news feature. A sentence near the bottom jumps at me and I know I must find her. We have enough people in common to form a small human bridge to get me to her. She once lived in Melbourne, no longer, but returns a few times a year. Email, Skype—she's on them. We meet, talk, soon it's clear: she is taking over something like a quarter of the book I'm writing. My heroine. The book. The book…

The book that I am writing. When I go searching for Vera I am convinced it will be done in twelve months or eighteen. Years fly: 20~~11-12-13-14-15-etc.~~. I console myself that books take as long as they take, the usual mantra, but it's different this time. This time it is like I have to choose between this book I'm writing and my conception of life. 'Most people,' Vera said to me one day, 'don't know who I am and I am not going to start telling them who I am because I can't be bothered. So there you are.'

There you are is Vera's way of ending stories.

As well as *that's how it goes*.

As well as *that was the end of the story*.

You think the wheels are beginning to turn on a story she's telling then you hear the screeching… *so there you are*. It's not obfuscation, and it's not like those stories can squash her, can undo her, she's able to handle them now and probably (this should give you a measure of her) always could. It's something else: the simultaneous, brutal pull of two forces perhaps. If a narrative of our life is something we weave during the day and unravel at night, 'loosening the woven cloth of the day in nocturnal trick' as Ovid wrote about Homer's Penelope, then there is in Vera—in the Vera I know—the urge towards the narrative and the urge away from it. It's in the memoir too. In the way the Polish story is told and the way the Australian story is not quite told, which is curious. You'd think trauma would make it the other way around.

Oh, yeah. The memoir. It comes out in 2015. *Vera: My Story*. A red/white/black cover with Vera on it looking like a gypsy queen. Fat cigar in her hand. It's half smoked. I think: I was so close. Then I remember: no, I wasn't.

The cover says 'with Robert Hillman'. Robert is Vera's materialised, declared ghost. It is his decision to put in the memoir behind-the-scenes marginalia including the times Vera's blowing hot air at him for not working faster, saying why is this taking so long, Robert, telling him she is not going to 'live forever', so you know, Robert.

I read this and think: she's addressing me not him.

The memoir is conceived, talked into existence, written, published, released, reviewed, moved from the front of the last still-standing bookshops to their densely shelved interiors, while I sit on my book with its twenty thousand unripe Vera words like Ilya Muromets on a pechka. I want to say to Robert: dear Robert, don't listen to her, listen to me, you are fast and good, miraculously so.

Vera says she can't be bothered telling people who she is except she is telling people, she is sharing her story, bothering to speak, maybe wishing she didn't have to while also finding some kind of charge in the telling, or maybe doing it almost automatically, speaking with her throat. Or perhaps speaking so as to protect some other truth she wishes to remain unnoticed, unsaid. The pleasures of attention are not to be discounted either. Vera is used to *that*. She has been *this*—the unmissable centre of every room—all her life. But these pleasures are not uncomplicated.

I go to the memoir's launch at the Readings bookshop branch in St Kilda. Robert is asking questions which Vera's answering politely though without the crackle often emitted by the riffing of a person's best stories and insights. I observe her looking around the room. As if expecting someone to be there. Someone who isn't. She refers, deadpan, to 'the Holocaust diet': eating weeds to survive. People laugh, relieved. I could listen forever to her slam the pleasure-denying-health-obsessed-first-world bullshit. Self-enforced hunger—to one starved as a child. Clean-living mania—to one whose people were supposed to be cleansed right out of their vermin-like existence. Self-mastery lite—when one's been through a historical catastrophe. The shop's back area is full. 'Are we done?' Vera says to Robert. She wants to be out of that chair.

The memoir's opening line: 'Outside, at a cafe in St Kilda, a new place at the back of the Prince of Wales, we're talking of murder.' *Murder* = Jews and WWII, *we're* = Robert and Vera, and years earlier—the memoir wasn't on the cards then—five women sat at a rectangular table in another St Kilda cafe. Vera had on a light, black dress hanging off thin-as-vermicelli straps. Green-and-black jewellery. A shawl. She looked better than good but not in a Taylorian—Gaborian way. Seventy-nine then and not an inch of her was caked-up or mumsy. 'Where'd you get such an exquisite shawl?' people were asking. 'From our ALDI supermarket, it's a great shawl for breastfeeding mothers,' she replied. Next time I see that shawl Jane will be wearing it. Jane—Vera's dear friend and former colleague at the ABC, where Vera worked first as a make-up artist, later as a producer.

Come to think of it I forget what anyone else wore that day—when I close my eyes, it's only Vera I see in colour—though I do remember coughing the place down, the prelude to a month-long pneumonia bout in the middle of a Melbourne summer, and I remember Vera with her veteran smoker's cough saying, 'You are really outcoughing me today,' which almost felt like a badge of honour—coughing like this, yet still up, out and about, living—since by then I had bumped into plenty of accounts of Vera's legendary staying powers. A friend in Byron Bay, where Vera moved after the ABC retrenched her, wrote to me: 'Had an outrageous night with Vera on Friday. She drank and smoked me under the table and we danced the evening away to her fabulous music collection.' This ability of Vera's to outlast—my friend was no lightweight—pretty much everyone was confirmed that day by Sophie. It was my first time meeting Sophie. 'Vera could always drink and smoke every day and be fine,' Sophie said. 'She still can. She says she is tired. These are words out of her mouth. But she can do it: drink, smoke, stay up, be OK.' Sophie is French not Polish but she lived in Poland as a young woman and speaks Polish with Vera. They met at a party in Melbourne long, long ago. How young they were then. From afar Vera looked Latin American. They got talking. Where are you from? Poland. In which city did you live? Warsaw. Which suburb? What street? Sophie must have told the story of meeting Vera a million times but she still made sure not to deny me its pop.

'Did you two live on *the same street*?' I asked.

'Better than that. Same building.'

Jane, draped in the breastfeeding shawl—she wasn't at the cafe on one of St Kilda's corners that morning but she'll be at Melbourne Jewish Writers Festival the year after the memoir's release: first row, Sophie on her left, the session will be called 'Vera Wasowski Tells It As It Is (As She Talks to Writer Maria Tumarkın)'. I'd come up with the title and blurb. I'd lobbied the festival producers to make me Vera's interlocutor. 'Pick me, please. I know her story. Know it back to front. I know too much.'

At the cafe Vera's phone kept ringing: people wanting to see her, cook her dinner, introduce her to someone. 'Vera,' said Sophie, 'has a talent for bringing people together and getting them to stay connected.' I told Sophie I was writing about Vera because something about her and her story made the by-now safe-seeming space of Holocaust testimonies dangerous again.

Dangerous felt right. Sophie knew what I was saying. She blessed me with her eyes.

Just about everyone who isn't family in the Australian part of Vera's memoir are Mirka Mora and Hazel Hawke types: famous. Jan was famous too: in Poland. Sophie is not famous. I don't think she is hurt about being omitted but I can't be sure. Theirs is a long, strong friendship. It feels tender, too. Young. At the launch, while people queue to buy the memoir Sophie and I discuss the reviewer in the *Australian* who three-quarters-canned it. Ridiculous review. She got Vera all wrong. Both of us like the book. The Polish part manages to do much more than replicate familiar-feeling tropes: idyllic childhood in Poland, prodigious child, yet another family of assimilated Jews oblivious to what's coming, the war, first Soviet soldiers, then German soldiers, marching into Lvov (Lviv, Lwów), ghetto, Aktions, childhood over, death everywhere, fear, hunger, survival, betrayal, more death, total eclipse of the world... The eclipse that will not end when the war ends. Everywhere in that part is Vera's bubble-pricking humour and her disdain for euphemisms. A refusal to make herself into something (a role model, a sage) she is not. Her inviolable gift for life. And appetite for it.

Something else the Wasowski/Hillman book does, or rather doesn't: it doesn't let readers walk away thinking they know what Vera lived through now that they have read the story and paid attention all the way through, now that they've agonised themselves an ulcer the size of a child's fist. Charlotte Delbo dealt with the question of knowing in 'O you who know'. *Dealt with*, i.e. made it impossible, as long as her poem is read, for anyone not possessed of first-hand experience of this kind of survival to tell themselves they are able to know what it was like:

> O you who know / did you know that you can see your mother dead / and not shed a tear /…O you who know / did you know that a day is longer than a year / a minute longer than a lifetime /…Did you know this / you who know.

'Oh well,' I say to Sophie, 'as for that hypothetical book of mine with the hypothetical Vera chapter it's by now a non-hypothetical total fuck-up. Fair enough too.'

'It is not over, Maria,' Sophie says. 'Maybe what you have to say is even more important now.'

We hug. What is it I have to say?

She is not angry with you, Sophie says when we meet again and sit in her parked car. Don't hide. She'll be in Melbourne for the Jewish writers festival to talk about the memoir. Get them to put her on with you.

I don't see what Sophie sees but can't figure out what to do with the Vera stuff inside of me. Thought I needed to just walk away. Am learning I can't. So I write an email. So I get a reply: 'Dear Maria—hello again! This is a wonderful idea. I need to discuss it with the rest of the committee to see how we fit this in… I will get back to you ASAP.'

In a few days the committee finds a way to *fit us in*.

My blurb, an excerpt:

> Wasowski's memoir … unlike any other book you're likely to read … sardonic, impolitic black humour … refusal to

abide by the conventions of living and writing about one's life.

My parents—they have read the memoir and want to hear Vera speak—are in the audience, and my daughter is there and my partner and my friend Tali who is on the festival's committee. Sophie, Jane. I consider mentioning my non-book, that hilarious failure, to be less like a stiff interlocutor and more a messy human in the spirit of Vera's low tolerance for polite society, but I don't. It's beside the point. Vera tells me before the session she's beginning to feel her age. Tired, she says. Can only take so much. Instead of a 'look at our hero Vera Wasowski' intro I describe a comedy routine the memoir starts with—Vera ranting to Robert about lycra-clad Melbourne bicycling bourgeoisie. Then moving swiftly to ranting about Melburnians' collective horror at the sight of a lit cigarette. Damn good start for a survivor memoir. I leave it up to Vera to see where she takes the war story. I see tears in Sophie's eyes. I spill water on my chair. Jane gets up and applauds Vera. The air in the room is just a little electric. You were right, Sophie. Once the session is over, I introduce Vera to my family, and I can see she will instantly forget their names and faces although she does notice my handsome partner.

Look at me—practically relishing my inability to tell Vera's story. We can tour together if Robert is too busy.

Herodotus tells a story of Histiaeus, who ruled Miletus in late sixth century BC and who, needing to communicate with Aristagoras, shaved a trusted slave's head, tattooed the message on the slave's scalp, and waited for the hair to grow back before sending him to Aristagoras. Aristagoras, in turn, shaved the slave's head to reveal Histiaeus's message encouraging him to revolt against the Persians, which, apparently, Aristagoras did. Steganography is the Greek word for the art of hiding messages—as opposed to, for instance, encrypting them. In Greek the word means 'concealed writing'. Most messages are hidden within other, larger, benign-seeming chunks of text. The existence of the secret message is a secret. We don't know to go looking. Perhaps telling and not-telling are not what we think they are. Perhaps experience could be placed in narrative for safekeeping, hidden in it, not to be buried, or rendered unknown, but to be preserved so as to be revealed in a different kind of story.

I go again through the memoir; it is on my bedside table seemingly permanently, durable yellow stickers a shortcut to particular bits—the nightclub story is there, wrapped up in a few lines, so's what her mother did to keep herself and Vera alive, so's what her father asked seven-year-old Vera to do… They've put it on the bloody back cover. I had to cancel myself as a writer, writing of that time. Couldn't bear my inadvertent embellishments—couldn't handle so much as my breathing—getting in there and re-punctuating her memory. Had to be Vera's words only. This next chunk she said to me, I kept till the near-end of my twenty thousand words on Vera:

> My mother was being looked after by my uncle, who was fucking her. The hiding place was available to us on condition that my uncle would get sexual comfort from my mother. Her condition was that she would bring me along. When it was safe I slept outside. During that time I developed my love of cockroaches because cockroaches were

walking over me all night as my mother was having intercourse with my uncle.

Then one day my father arrived. The transport failed; the ghetto was closed; he had nowhere to go. We were the only people he had contact with. And my uncle was throwing him out. They had this big conversation in German. I could hear, '*Heraus! Heraus!* Get out!' But my father, who looked very Jewish, couldn't leave the hiding place because he would have been killed. By then we all wore bags of poison: my father wanted to make sure we had that 'little out'. I wore that bag always. We didn't have quick poison anymore, you couldn't get cyanide, so we had heaps and heaps of sleeping powder. My father gave me instructions—if someone gets hold of me and there is no way out, ask for a glass of water.

There was a lot of that powder. He obviously had taken half of it with a glass of water and was in a coma for three days in that hiding hole where we all were. Then he woke up and I was going to see how he was going. You could smell his urine. He asked me for a glass of water. I knew exactly what I was doing. I went and got him a glass of water from the kitchen, crawled back into the hiding place, gave him the glass of water.

He said that I was not going to have him anymore, just the mother. And that he was not going to take me to the Sorbonne anymore when I grow up because he wasn't going to be there. And then he died. He died and my uncle who I absolutely hate till this day, although I know you shouldn't hate anyone, and this other Polish fellow who was hiding us, wrapped his body in a blanket, dug a hole in the cellar, and buried my father. When the Russians started bombing Lvov we had to go into the cellar to hide and I was very aware I was standing on my father.

When my father killed himself, not a word was spoken. It happened and that's how it was. For the rest of my mother's life, both of us were pretending that none of it happened, pretending that everything was normal, when absolutely nothing was normal. That was the end of the story.

I kept this till the near-end of my twenty thousand words because I wanted to dissolve into black, into white. I wanted to kick floorboards out from under my readers' feet, make them rethink everything I told them about Vera, all that they had come to imagine and to believe—now that they knew what happened to her at age seven. That was then. And now? Now I am the one who has to rethink everything because Vera's life is not a story I can tell, and yet it is its non-storyness that feels increasingly essential somehow, in need of being noticed.

We, soft-fleshed denizens of the West, have come to rely on a certain image of a Holocaust survivor (and other kinds of survivor too) taken over by their moral and emotional compulsion to testify *lest the world forgets*, sometimes like Levi, Borowski, Frankl or the non-Jewish Delbo (although Delbo held off publishing) immediately after the war, more often later, once the world's plucked the cherry stones out of its ears and begun listening. But a just-as-powerful compulsion inside survivors steers towards silence. Survival leaves you knowing both testimony and silence as tainted choices, each riddled equally with despair.

You MUST speak because how else will what happened to you and your people be known as the monstrosity it was, as the end of the world that it is, how else to turn it to anathema, make it an impossibility in the future? You see how unthinkably fast the world's memory is fading, hear more and more 'no, it didn't happen that way'. You must speak because the act of speaking, the narrative you make and remake with each telling, is what will keep you alive, what you'll hang on to, because this narrative covers, incompletely, too bad, the hole inside you. You must speak because if you don't, they win. If you don't, you have stopped fighting, given up.

You must NOT speak because it's with only a few fellow survivors that these conversations are properly possible—the telling and the listening do not feel so piercingly unreal. As if it is about someone else. You must not speak because what you know is impossible to bring into language, it's beyond transmitting, and whatever you can say is only a tiny bit of it and by saying it and letting them think it's the whole thing you are betraying the memory of those who cannot speak, or be silent, for themselves. You must not speak because this speaking exhausts you, empties you out, the burden of remembering and testifying is too much, the tyranny of narrative—too much—you do not wish to go back there again and again, and for what? You must not speak because your life is much bigger than this, you've made it so, beaten the odds. You must not speak because you have done more than enough speaking.

Elie Wiesel was interviewed in 1978, the conversation appearing in a 1984 *Paris Review*.

INTERVIEWER: For ten years you waited until you were ready to write about the Holocaust in your first book, *Night*.

WIESEL: I didn't want to use the wrong words. I was afraid that words might betray it. I waited. I'm still not sure that it was the wrong move, or the right move, that is, whether to choose language or silence.

A minute or two later…

INTERVIEWER: What do you mean you didn't want to write those books?

WIESEL: I didn't want to write a book on the Holocaust… I had to. It wasn't voluntary. None of us wanted to write. Therefore when you read a book on the Holocaust, written by a survivor, you always feel this ambivalence. On one hand, he feels he must. On the other hand, he feels … if only I didn't have to.

Vera via Robert in the memoir…

'You're a Jew, you survive the ghetto: you tell the story for the rest of your life. You have to believe that it matters. Poor Primo Levi, the tiled floor rushing up at him, facing what the Nazis could not achieve: his death. And why? Because what Robert wants to hear from me Levi had ceased to believe meant anything to listeners, to readers, to anyone… Someday someone will say to me, "*The Holocaust?* Is that a movie?", and like Primo Levi I will see the floor speeding towards my face.'

If life were different, if I could write books like normal people, I'd have had Vera all to myself.

First my book comes out.

After that, a respectful amount of time later, her memoir with Robert.

The way writers do, I'd have slotted the parts into place for maximum impact hoping the readers might be taken by the life of another. I would have looked at Vera's life, and thought—

and said to myself, and out loud—*what an amazing story. (Get a load of that!)*

This space I ended up in between the telling and the not-telling I would not have chosen in a million years.

'Better a titmouse in the hand than a crane in the sky'— odd-sounding in English but in Russian it is one of those commonplace expressions featuring a commonplace Russian bird. You grow up with these birds and sayings flitting around you. Most cultures have a version of the saying. Sparrows and pigeons, hens and eagles, chicken, geese; in English it's 'a bird in the hand is worth two in the bush'. A human life is often written about as if it is *in the hand* of whoever is doing the writing. It isn't. It is always the two birds in the bush. Which is to say, it cannot be *captured*, that deceptively friendly English word for speaking of other people's lives, and it cannot be fully *grasped*, another faux-friendly word for going deep into people's worlds. Life of a child survivor? That's more like four birds in the bush. Oh, come on, you know what I am saying: it's only right that this one flew away.

• • •

Scientists say childhood amnesia is a thing and it happens around seven. Children forget their early memories. As adults we may later remember those moments, whole honeycombs of them sometimes—most people say their earliest memory dates from when they were three, four—but we'll remember them the way a not-yet-seven child remembers. As sensations. These memories tend to be physical, emotional, visceral, without narrative. 'At seven,' Paul Valent is telling me, 'you start remembering like an adult, going back in your mind to a particular moment and remembering it in sort of an adult way.' Seven marks the beginning of autobiographical memory: memory that organises, rather than obliquely underpinning, our sense of self. Except with trauma where none of it works like any of that.

Psychologist Vicki Gordon tells me of a conversation with a man who as a child survived the Holocaust. The man, a big-shot doctor, remembers little from his early childhood. The traumatic episodes he can remember with clarity.

On late-night radio is Dasia Black, who survived WWII in open hiding, living with a Polish Christian family as an Aryan child, praying to the right god, kneeling low, clutching so tight-ly her new identity that for a while she could not remember her real name. Her parents died early in the war. Eventually her real uncle and aunt adopted her, the three of them finishing up in Australia. Black doesn't like the word 'survivor'. It's got 'some tinge to it', she explains to the radio host, 'of strength, of something special, whereas it was simply circumstance. My parents were not survivors, does it make them any less?'

Children of WWII were not seen as survivors until the 1980s. Parents of those children—parents who made it alive to the war's end—they were the survivors and even that re-alisation took its sweet time taking root. Then in the '70s the idea emerged of a second generation, children born after the war who were, as was often said, carrying the unhealable scars without sustaining the wounds. For them, wrote Eva Hoffman, a second-generationer herself, their family's past was 'a sort of supercondensed pellet of primal information ... from which everything else grows, or explodes, or follows, and which it takes a lifetime to unpack and decode'.

That was them and meantime child survivors—alive during the war—were afloat, largely. Afloat for four decades. It was believed they could not remember what happened. And believed they, burdened by neither memory nor knowledge of the nature or scale of what they'd lived through, couldn't be possessed by the war in the same permanent way as the adults around them. Believed wrongly (obviously—that much has been worked out and owned up to).

Dasia Black is being asked what a young child—she was three and a half when the war started—could actually understand. Grown-up Black's a child psychologist. So the question is deliberately double barrelled.

A child understands to be quiet, she replies, and to hide when a Gestapo raid is on, how to pretend to be someone else, do anything not to displease the family that's taken her in, understands how to walk away from her parents and continue walking while every instinct, every molecule, every piece of gravity pushes her back to them. What Orpheus couldn't do once he left the underworld—keep walking and looking ahead when his whole reason for being, his Eurydice, was behind him; a child could do that.

'What could a child like this remember?' Phillip Adams on the radio says to Dasia Black.

'Most of it,' she answers.

'I had the childhood I had,' Vera was saying to me one day, 'and therefore I embarked on my life fearless. And therefore I have done whatever I have done with my life the way I really wanted to.'

A society like ours that sees the protection of children as its first moral necessity might be well served recognising children's vulnerability as originating in their capacity, not their incapacity, for knowledge and action. This capacity—extraordinary at times, especially in the face of a catastrophe, private or public—has limitations but these limitations are often not what we think they are.

One day in 1942 two men in trenchcoats approached Paul Valent and his parents on a Budapest street. Not long before, in the night, Paul, his mother and his father crossed the border from Slovakia into Hungary. Four-year-old Paul was riding on his father's shoulders. He could not see others in their group but he could hear whispers that would die down every time dogs barked in the distance. Paul didn't know his father's business had been confiscated and in their country Jews, which included most of his extended family, were being deported to concentration camps but he did know that their walk, as he wrote sixty years later in a memoir, *In Two Minds*, meant 'life and death'. 'I just knew I had to be totally quiet. I knew not to think or feel.' And when in Budapest a new identity—Christian, Hungarian, stretching back generations—was drilled into him, together with admonitions not to ever let anyone see his penis, he knew to cling to that identity with everything he had. 'I understood in my marrow that if I slipped up there would be unimaginable consequences. I was only four, and I did not slip up for three years.'

Two trenchcoated men. A sunny day. Paul's parents told him to wait. They were going with 'these two gentlemen' to 'buy some ice-cream' and would be back in ten minutes. They did not come back in ten minutes or ten days. As they walked down the street they didn't turn to glance, to give their son a sign, a look. (How many stories like this end well? Point one percent would you say? This one ended well—Paul's mum and dad were arrested, sent back to Slovakia, put on a cattle train to Auschwitz, taken off the train at the last minute because a relative, still free, bribed the guards; they found Paul after a few months and survived the war together, passing as Aryans. Ending well doesn't quite take into account the mother's eyes—'yearning, pitying, and distant'—after the three of them were reunited, or the father's subsequent death in his prime from cancer, as well as adult Paul's own wearying detachment, that emotional numbness psychiatrists like to write their books about. Still the Valents were ones who had 'a good war', in Hoffman's haunting words, 'hounded only by fear of discovery rather than by physical torments and indignities'.)

In his memoir Valent tells of another moment: he's in his fifties, a father of three, renowned psychiatrist, writer, founder of a child survivors of the Holocaust group in Melbourne. He is with his son in Hungary. Third trip back since the war—was here just the year before, in Slovakia too, with his daughter, they found the house that was their hiding place (still standing) and went to Auschwitz where most of their family was killed. This time Paul with his son returns to the hiding house and a different urge overwhelms him. He wants to find the street, the spot, where he watched the four figures disappear, knowing to let them go, knowing to not say a word. He doesn't know the name of the street. All he has is an image of two men in hats and trenchcoats talking to his parents. By accident he sees a book in a shop window. Sees the book's title—a name in it triggers something in him. His parents talked a lot about a street with this name. He checks. The street exists; it's really close to where they must have lived.

He hurries to the street. Reminds himself he was a child not an adult then. He crouches, lets himself go, allows his body to remember. He checks. A well-known ice-cream shop was at the end of the street.

This is why his parents must have thought to say ice-cream.

He goes to the spot, squats, remembers being left, remembers his mother not looking back, remembers thinking what have I done wrong? Then he knows—'my mother could not have looked back, because whether she had smiled or cried, I would have run after her.' The greatest betrayal of his life was an act of purest love. He understands then that the child who knew so much and didn't slip up, not once, did not until half a century later know the most important thing.

A child can know to be quiet, know a walk across a border into a country covered in darkness is life-or-death business, know never to let their real name squeak out or let anyone see them naked. A child simply cannot know perhaps that a mother walking away is the mother saving their life. Maybe only an adult can know this.

And then the war ends. Your life's no longer *theirs*. And then what. The challenge of the living, writes Robert Krell, another child-survivor-turned-psychiatrist, becomes 'how to survive having survived'. Except what does it mean for a child exposed to evil to feel like a child again, if that's what surviving one's survival at least partly entails? If feeling like a child means not carrying, not yet, the full burden of protecting your borders as a sovereign being should we be wishing, with fervour, for traumatised children to feel like children again? If this feeling's the one that makes children vulnerable should we fight for it, like it's an unalienable good? Should we consider its denial (or impossibility) a deep failing by the world?

'When we went into hiding,' Vera says to me, 'I stopped being a child. I understood I had to take responsibility for my own being, my own existence.'

—Did you ever feel like a child after the war ended?

—Nah.

—It was gone completely?

—I think so.

Wisława Szymborska, the second Polish poet, Milosz was the other, to be awarded a Nobel Prize in the twentieth century had a poem called 'Autotomy'. Autotomy—when animals amputate a part of themselves in self-defence like the holothurian does in the poem:

In danger, the holothurian cuts itself in two.
It abandons one self to a hungry world
and with the other self it flees.

One part is salvation, hope. The other is beyond salvation. One part is allowed to die so the other can reconstitute itself and grow into a living whole. A survivor is a holothurian. To say that is to say survival is not the opposite of death. It may in some sense be much closer to death than to life. Years after the war, Vera's war I'm talking about, Mado—Charlotte Delbo's friend and fellow survivor—would say to Delbo, 'I died in Auschwitz, and no one knows it,' and Delbo herself would write, 'Can one come out of there alive? No. It wasn't possible.'

A survivor learns how to be alive and dead. A child survivor is a particular kind of survivor: an expert in doubleness. And a child who survived in hiding like Vera did is its own category.

Vicki Gordon interviewed hidden child survivors—her parents were two—half a century later, noticing a certain 'cut-offness'. A persistent matter-of-factness in many of her interviewees. A dryness, lack of 'psychological depth'. At times, when the adult could look at herself as the child—compassionate adult seeing suffering child and feeling hard for that child who is them and not them—emotions broke through, but this was the adult not child feeling. Hidden children survive by remaining silent, invisible. Not asking for anything, not crying, never crying. Any emotion could deplete reserves of psychological strength. Expression of distress or fear in open hiding under a false identity could out you as a Jew. Inability to contain oneself could lead to discovery. Once, when the tape recorder was finally off, a child survivor said to Gordon, 'I know what you want from me but you are not going to get it even if you sit here all day.'

'I went to a palm reader in Byron Bay,' Vera tells me on Skype, 'and he said he hadn't seen genes like that, such protection.'

The reason Vera ended up in Byron Bay post-ABC was because her son lived there—her late son now, his death from a heart attack in a sauna came out of nowhere, he was fifty-something.

'My son,' Vera says, 'was an extraordinary fellow who at the age of eighteen rejected us, saying I do not care about your refrigerator and your car and I'm going to go bush. Completely different fellow to us. I could understand him more when I started studying Buddhism after being retrenched from the

ABC.' Retrenchment: may sound trivial next to what else she had to live through.

It was not. You start off your life feeling special. Such a precocious child your father will take you to the Sorbonne. Maybe not now, not while war's on, but even now Soviet soldiers, occupying Lvov, listen to you play piano and want to send you to study music in Moscow. You're that good, beautiful too, then you learn you're nothing—the lesson couldn't be clearer—until out of that obliteration of self you build yourself again and come to believe you're special two times over, a phoenix. And then they tell you *you don't work here anymore.* Which to your ears sounds like *you're nothing.*

'I am not someone who walks around saying please understand, I had a terrible life. I am not. Some lives go this way. Other lives go another way.' Feeling down does hit Vera, time to time, and when it happens a Jewish friend of hers will say, 'Vera, be happy no Nazis are at the front door.' She thinks about it and feels happy. Wallowing, dwelling, moaning, sniffles—not for her. Moving forward, moving on, living, loving whatever can be loved in the life you live, devouring, delighting—her verbs.

'I had that childhood. Didn't have any close friendships. Was very direct. I didn't have any patience for stupidity already then. I was never too conventional. When I was seventeen, eighteen, I began having an enormous success with men, with young men, because they saw I was so different and it would be worthwhile to make contact with me.'

Having that childhood meant knowing: no guarantees possible: it could happen again. People, trained parrots, chanting *Never again! Never!* when if you lived through what she lived

through, you'd see the falseness of that, and then when the
never-again happened again the chanters would be blindsid-
ed. Struck hapless. Too late to stop it by the time they catch
up. The heavyweight Australian names Vera likes to drop—
the 'top people', 'elite', just like in her Warsaw circle—aren't
merely symbolic of her rejection of Australia's petty bourgeoisie, or proof of her not betraying the self she forged in postwar
Warsaw. They have a practical purpose. If need be, they can
protect her. At least some will be in a position to keep her safe.
She still has a way of making people fuss around her. I don't
think she does anything in particular to encourage the fuss. It's
in the forcefield.

'It is like the Jewish god gave Vera the supreme order to
survive,' Sophie says. 'Everything else comes from it.'

As Vera and I talk, as my book slides, drags, grows stalac-
tites and slips further instead of gets closer, the Royal Commission into Institutional Responses to Child Sexual Abuse be-
gins and gathers pace. Every day are reports detailing cases of
children abused with brutality, impunity, elaborately over large
tracts of time, as recent as a few years ago. On TV news you
glimpse these child/adults—looking eaten away by the past,
saying 'pain builds up like rust in a metal waterpipe'. When I
am walking the streets of my city I cannot stop myself imagining abused children hiding in adult bodies. I don't want to
check the statistics. I'm sure the stats are staggering. On a bad
day, reading report after report and my mind goes to imagining my children violated then my jaw locks, all the talk about
people's reclaiming of safety, self, soul and family wrecked by
abuse feels like pissing in the ocean. 'Some call sexual abuse
"soul murder", it's a real destruction of a person's value and

dignity,' Paul Valent says to me. 'Generationally too, it inter-
feres with love.'

Why in a child-centric world the violation of children
should be so endemic, and what violation produces across a
lifetime and beyond, are questions the legalistic language 'gross
breach of children's rights' and journalistic language 'breaking of the human spirit' and therapeutic language 'damage to
children's psychosocial, sexual, spiritual development' cannot
get us close to. Innocence—talking about that as the thing defining of children, and which trauma rips out of them... I like
how an Australian philosopher, Joanne Faulkner, deals with innocence. Three big problems she says: first it's a self-serving
adult fantasy; also it makes adults give up on children believed
to be no longer in possession of their innocence; finally it stops
children participating in an ethical and civic life.

Innocence—Vera's take on it in the memoir. 'Modern psychologists say that children usually think of death as a tem-
porary and reversible thing, that a child's consciousness is not
equipped to deal with the permanence of death. Not the children of the Lvov ghetto. We know that you can be alive in the
morning and dead in the afternoon.'

Every Tom or Jill in a drycleaned suit can quote Dietrich
Bonhoeffer. 'Test of the morality of a society is what it does for
its children.' Impossible to debate. But what of the adults made
as children to witness and endure things monstrous, intolerable? What are they owed? They are on every full train, in every
medium-size workplace, child survivors in grown-up bodies. If
they care to self-identify, oh, we've got a job for you—you be
Guardian of Memory, you be Witness, you be indefatigable
Truth Teller, you be Moral Lightning Rod. Won't you, dear

survivor? Don't let the rest of us forget or dream it never happened. Walk in circles in this public square over there, won't you?

'Is *that* what you are going to do to us?'—Imre Kertész (nine when WWII started) who wrote *Kaddish for an Unborn Child*—'How could we survive something like this, and understand it, too?'

I speak to a woman, J, abused in every way you could abuse a child and who testified at the Royal Commission. How strong she is and how hurt. It's not just the life she lived, it's what she is. J tells me she regrets testifying. Nothing happened after her testimony, or not yet anyway, and the wound is wide open, it's tougher the second time around to live with it bleeding over everything. She tried so hard to get herself together. Particularly for her kids who didn't know anything till recently. Now J is wondering if she'll get sick all over again and make others around her sick. And reliving the injustice of it, who'd want that, and for nothing. There is a moment in our conversation— am I torturing her with my questions? should I stop? better to continue?—when something happens, shifts. I don't know what. She writes a day or two later, 'Hey, Maria, just wanting to tell you at the end of our chat you said "do you think if someone had said you have carried the burden for such a long time…"'—not exact words I know but while you were still talking my mind went into a mad crazy time … hard to explain … anyway wow the word burden really hit me.'

'Burden' hit me too, reading J's email. Burden brings other words with it: weight, carrying, lifting, putting down, exhaustion. Words to add to the familiar ones: testimony, witness, listening, telling, lest we forget, story, transmission.

Putting burden at the centre. The body—all of it—moves to the centre too. I think, shit, it's what we actually do, isn't it? We—writers. We lift a bit off. We carry some corner of it some of the way. We ask without asking, 'Would anything make it lighter?' We ask, 'What would make you rest for a bit?' Kookaburras we are not, more like limping horses and donkeys.

Vera likes to repeat she is an 'unresolved walking trauma' and I can tell she particularly savours the word 'unresolved'.

• • •

Vera goes back to Lvov (Lwów, Lviv). Her grandson Pani, who lives in London, joins her. We Skype a few months later. 'The trip was so long ago I've forgotten about it,' Vera says.

First Warsaw, then to Lvov. 'Lvov,' she says, 'is a wonderful town. You told me you've been there, haven't you? No? Anyway we were in Lvov and we found the address in the ghetto of where we stayed. So we went there. Everyone took lots of photographs apart from me because I don't take photographs. They still haven't sent me any. And I located the block of flats where we lived before the war. The building is still standing. So this was Lvov. The weather was wonderful.'

Skype is hissing. We disconnect and reconnect, turn the video off.

'When we were on our way to the Jewish archives it was the first time since the Holocaust, would you believe, that I had tears in my eyes. I couldn't cry all my life. But this was all right, like a cleansing thing. I gave them my parents' names and my grandparents' and so on and I thought it'd take them weeks but on Friday—we were leaving on Saturday—they called us.

"Come within half an hour," the woman said, "and I'll guide you how to get there." This was the hiding place. And the fucking taxi driver held a big conference. Whole area, he said, had been done up. And the house where we were hiding was bricked up but it was still there. I saw it. So there we are. And then we went to Berlin. Berlin was another story altogether. I got tickets to Daniel Barenboim conducting even though the show was sold out. The guy who got us tickets offered for me to meet Barenboim. And I said, "What the fuck for? To go backstage and shake hands?" There wasn't much point.'

Was it hard being in Lvov? First time back as an adult. 'I thought I might be traumatised,' Vera says, 'but I wasn't. Nothing was difficult. Wonderful restaurants. Excellent coffee. The difference between the Jewish population prewar and now is the only thing. And that's all I can tell you, darling. Traditionally Lvov was an intellectual person's town. Big university. There was a writers festival on when we visited. I met a fellow who was there for the festival and who fell in love with me. Born in Lvov, lives in the USA. He gave me his book with the most wonderful inscription. That was it. It was speedy. It was quick. So there you are.'

There I am. 20~~11 12 13 14 15 16 17 etc.~~18.

YOU CAN'T ENTER THE
SAME RIVER TWICE

2.

WE WERE READING the Soviet encyclopedia in a park. The one from when Stalin was alive. Your mother's copy. The Father of All Nations was apparently a great scientist too on top of his other skills. Just couldn't help being gifted in every striving and endeavour. We were laughing. Our crazy country with its crazy history. The craziest ever. Broad daylight, people everywhere. They surrounded us. One of them must have had a ring. I'd see a male hand with a ring on a tram or a trolleybus for weeks after and I'd flinch. My parents said to each other, maybe they wanted me to hear, 'This is why we are doing this.'

OK, memory has been kind with me on this one: two Jewish girls went walking through a park, having brought along a fat philosophical dictionary from the 1960s. There was much that was absurd in that dictionary and they were planning to laugh their time away in the tree shade. In the middle of their merriment they were approached by two or three young, not entirely sober, scumbags. Maybe the scumbags didn't take to the girls' laughter, maybe the girls' non-Slavic features weren't to scumbags' liking. Could have easily been a two-in-one. There may have been some 'ideological' bickering between us and them—that bit I don't remember. What I re-

member, remember it acutely,
is a feeling of powerlessness,
a feeling of being nothing,
when they hit you over the
head in front of me, and the
sentence you said on the way
home: 'This happened so I
could be cured of any nos-
talgia for the motherland.'
I remember—curious—the
precise place on Sumskaya
where you said these words.
Right on the intersection with
Petrovsky Street.

3.

Sometimes after school we simply couldn't say goodbye and
so we stood under the tree on Chernyshevskaya Street in our
stupid servile uniforms. The brown of the winter uniform was
like [complete the sentence]. It was like decomposing earth-
worms eating chocolate spongecake deep in the mud. I want
to say we stood under that tree for hours but I am conscious
perceptions of time are age-specific blah blah, context-specific
blah triple blahdee blah. Anyway it felt like hours. Or we'd
say goodbye, fly home—yours, stuffed with other families, was
closer to the tree; I had to walk past the bookshop, Akadem-
kniga, where your mum worked to get to mine—and call each
other on the phone straight away. Now I make faces when I
talk on the phone to make it tolerable. I am one of those people
who prefer either face-to-face or email: total co-presence or
total separation in time and space.

4.

Your sixteenth. My flowers, as tall as you, maybe taller. Hugging, giggling. The flowers, we said, look like 'drunk Olympic swimmers'. *Cruel optimism*—have you heard this expression?

5.

Nina Sergeevna, useless as a teacher, but oh those dark curls and eyes. Dressed well too. Don't laugh. Such a bitch, though. Determined to not let me sit next to you. Every class she would send me to the last row where no one ever sat. It became a ritual. And you, you were annoyed with me, not her, weren't you? You wanted less fuss, less drama, you thought my defiance was becoming ridiculous. What exactly was I fighting for? I don't know what possessed me, but I wasn't going to give up. I was going to go on like this forever. Like a self-appointed Sisyphus. Twice a week, planting my feet next to your desk waiting for her bored voice to call me out.

Who is Nina Sergeevna? Not our English teacher by chance? Can't remember much about her. For some reason all English teachers at that time were these arrogant damsels, dressed to the nines and dazzling of manicure. At least she knew the language.

I thought I'd keep going till someone dies or school ends or she gives in or I black out.

6.

Sometimes after school we simply couldn't say good-bye. Or we'd say goodbye, fly home—one flight of stairs for you, one flight for me, one older sister to 'neutralise' for you, one older sister to 'neutralise' for me, parents at work and won't be home for hours, best if sisters are busy with love entanglements—and call each other on the phone straight away. Now I am one of those people who think 'Who is dead?' if a phone rings in the evening.

What year was it when you called after searching for me up and down the internet? 2003? 2005? I don't remember which out of a dozen nomadic rented flats I was in when your phone call found me. I did not have a mobile then. My entire adult life, I've only had four phones. First computer—got that in 2008. Ugly, huge, with a round-eye monitor. Junk really. Made me so happy. Do you remember how I would write to you at home, save it on a flash disk, run to an internet cafe to send it off.

7.

Just the other day my father sent me an academic article in which a literary scholar discusses our (yours and my) friendship (among other things). The scholar commends me for 'unashamed embrace' of 'big emotions'. Between the lines (but not disapprovingly): how very non-Anglo Saxon. She cites examples of my 'emotional intensity', symptomatic, she writes, of the time and the place of my childhood and adolescence. Terrible, soggy tra-ti-ta-ta passages from Book 3. Am I a chest beater? Looks like it. Also, I wonder if painters' eyes burn like this too when they land, in passing, on an old canvas.

8.

I am looking through them now and can see all your letters from those first years—1990, 91, 92—and after that: nothing. Did you stop writing to me? Did everything stop? Was THAT when you decided it was all over? I remember: *the past is all we have and it's not enough.*

'I dug up somewhere Tsvetaeva's diaries. Just listen to this:

"To love—is to see a person the way God intended him and his parents failed to make him.

To not love—is to see a person as his parents made him.

To fall out of love: is to see, instead of him, a table, a chair."'

9.

(We were best friends.) I wrote about us. I wrote about us sitting on a park bench with an old Soviet encyclopedia on our laps. I wrote about us remembering this together, in situ, nineteen years later:

'No,' says Sasha, 'there were only three guys who hassled us but one of them hit you over the head.'

'How is it that I have tripled the numbers and managed to forget a blow to my head?'

'Go figure,' says Sasha.

I wrote about that day, D-Day, sweet sixteenth, your coming of age:

If I could have given her a hundred of these flowers, if I could have surrounded her with a forest of them, I would have.

I don't know that this is what I meant to do but I put us on the public record.

10.

CNN Live, Stuart Loory to Larry King:

Larry, you can't imagine the scene in that room. Mikhail Gorbachev walked in, looked very relaxed, sat down at the table, in front of him was a simple green folder with a few sheets of paper. They were his speech and they were the

'Hello, my disappearing one... With every day you're becoming further away and I am drowning in all the trivial bullshit around me. I am frightened that I am losing you, losing the only REAL thing I had. I am frightened, you hear me? Of course you hear me. You always hear

documents with which he was going to sign away the power... I have in my hand [lifts and shows to camera] the pen that he used to abdicate the presidency of the USSR. After his speech he had to sign the document and his pen didn't work. Tom Johnson, the president of CNN, was standing at the table. He gave this pen to Mikhail Gorbachev. Gorbachev signed. Tom asked him for the pen back and he's allowed me to bring it over here to show to your viewers, Larry.

me when I am calling you. If you didn't, it'd be a colossal cruelty on His part. Is it not enough for Him that I haven't seen you in fourteen months? And you know what's most frightening? I am getting used to living without you. The first months I just wept. I thought I was not going to make it. "Time heals" sounds like a bitterly cutting joke. I don't want it to heal me... OK, no more of this, but ... just one last thing—let it hurt.'

(*Letter prices have gone up; on the envelope—three additional, identical stamps, a harp and quill in green and grey.*)

11.

Larisa Petrovna, our Year 4 classroom teacher, used to smoke behind a tree. She lived alone. Her hiding and smoking, smoking while hiding, was the only thing about her I found interesting—stains on

Your sister came to the graduation, she was visiting if you remember, and hung a pearl necklace round my neck and gave me an Otto catalogue (fashion catalogues from Germany were beyond cool then)

her fingers, her teeth pickled in the subterranean smoke, what's so interesting about that? Had she smoked in the classroom, that'd be interesting. She was short, with the short hair, skinny. She taught algebra and geometry: I was good at the first, no good at the second (rotating a 3D shape in my head? Ciò non è possibile! Sorry!). I was the first in Larisa Petrovna's class to *swim to the other shore*.

as a gift. I wore a skirt made out of my sister's wedding dress, a modest white jacket, a black top. Plus pearls, your sister's. Mum said I looked touchingly pure, an innocent amid all the overdressed, overdone girls of our class. The graduation itself—grey, grey, grey. Larisa Petrovna (dear and beloved) got smashed (to smithereens) and at 4 a.m. dragged us all to meet the sunset in Dzerzhinsky Square. She talked utter nonsense there and then everyone, pissed off and sleepy, went their separate ways.

12.
(We were best friends. I wrote about us, mea culpa-style too…):
I had not seen my childhood friends in Ukraine for almost two decades; to them, and especially to my best friend who turned sixteen on the day etc etc… *nothing short of a* etc etc etc… *It took nineteen years for me* etc *and I was coming back so I could write a* etc etc…

In some talk I gave I said I used my daughter, twelve at the time, as a 'human shield' to be able to go back. I didn't say 'go back to you'.

13.

Years after her immigration Dina Rubina popped into a Moscow bookshop: 'It was a terrible shock. I realised that all books had already been written. They had all been released. There were so many of them already that there was absolutely no need to write any more. If you decided to write something, you had to be prepared to wage a war for your reader. You had to be prepared not to hold back.' We watch Rubina's interview on the same day—me (t)here, you (t)here.

14.

We were best friends. I wrote about us and about how we thought it was the end of the line. Except, a month earlier the Berlin Wall came down, a year and a bit later our country 'collapsed' (the word used by authorised purveyors of that tale) and it no longer seemed so absolute that Those Who Left would never sit around the same table with Those Who Stayed Behind. We saw each other again nineteen years after that, in 2008, beforehand you said, 'Let's not. There is no need,

I told you to meet me outside my alma mater—Kharkiv State Academy of Culture on Bursatskiy Descent. I got there half an hour early, went first to the dean's office. Tears, my hands were trembling. I managed to gather myself and come out almost composed (at least, so I thought). Then: circling the city, joined by the cheerful Italian Marina, our foray into the Palace of Pioneers, photos there, ice-cream in a cafe, you and her exchanging your autographed books, trip

no point.' I said, 'Give me an hour.'

to the other side of the city in a dirty minibus, tea and cake, as if in a dream… My ridiculous boots with 10cm heels clearly not intended for long walks around the city… I would have worn them three/ four times my whole life, no more than that! They are still hanging in a storeroom from a carefully sewn-on thread (so that the shaft with the hand-made ornament wouldn't get crumpled, for Christ's sake). My next night, sleepless, was in someone else's kitchen (you remember where I lived and who with), an almost empty pack of cigarettes (whole week's ration! shit!).

15.
I would meet people in my new life and they would know about you (ask questions etc.) and I would be startled, wrongfooted— how on earth…?

16.
Those photos from 2008, I deleted them. I would have gladly cut you out and kept you but it's a bad omen. It's my face I can't bear to look at. My face twisted by the pain of that time.

17.

'Hello, my friend. The cold is back. About minus five outside and inside plus fifteen, no more. In the kitch-en and bathroom—plus ten. Getting undressed and washing yourself is a heroic feat. Once it hits minus ten outside it'll be twelve inside and eight in the kitchen. You have to beat the shower gel out of its bottle then warm it in the palm of your hand with your breath. The house is impossible to heat. A metre-long space under the kitchen floor is colonised by the travelling wind. The pocket under the floor should have rocks, gravel, but it's been left empty. I've come up with a little trick— when I feel frozen to the bone, I go to the kitchen for ten/fifteen minutes. Coming back into "the warmth" of the room is such a relief. The contrast does wonders, not for long but for long enough. I haven't been scared of death for a long time unlike my mum who is regularly transmitting her fear —can't stand it when she does it. The fear I feel is that of the meaninglessness of my time here. Like, what the hell has this been about?'

18.

Friday nights my son goes to his father. *What if he doesn't come back?* I really think like that. Five years of Fridays. I tried: drinking, sleeping, working, walking. We get him back on Monday, by Wednes-day/Thursday he is finally at peace. Friday rolls in like an army.

Saturdays are the worst. All the fears and worries fall on me like a wad of snow. It's been like that for ten years already. This Saturday I was in bed all day, couldn't even wash my hair. Got up once in a while and trudged to the kitchen, swaying side to side, for some tea. Spent all day

watching war movies. Still,
I'd rather feel like an 'empty
bamboo' than a 'bowl of sem-
olina porridge'.

19.

You recommend poet Vera Pavlova. From her notebook (published, transl. in English)—
'Reader: So you want me to feel as if *I* were reading a letter
addressed to someone else?
Poet: I want you to feel as if I had read a letter addressed to you
by someone else and am shamelessly quoting from it.'

I recommend poet Wisława Szymborska.

20.

'Friends reveal who they are
in hardship'—imbibed in
infancy, absorbed pre-cog-
nitively. You too, right? Sits
there like a brick in your head.
Along with 'the cat knows
whose meat it has eaten'. And
if you're not sure vis-a-vis a
particular person, take them
'high into the mountains'
[V.S. Vysotsky]; also, once   The dream I had last night:
off the mountain, remem-   we are swimming in a river,
ber to go jointly through a   a pretty dirty river, probably

'pound of salt' [people, *volk*]. Note how it's salt—white poison—not grains, say, or life-extending sorrel, and high in the mountains, by the way, the scrutinised are allowed to act annoyed and withdrawn as long as, when you start falling, they 'moan' [V.S. Vysotsky] but grab arms, legs and hold tight. And if not up in the mountains, then down into a forest with partisans we go—Alexievich says the only language we know how to speak is the language of war—can you trust this person with your life? Do a mental experiment and you'll know. Is this normal? Too late for me, regardless. The most I can muster is a grain of salt about the pound of salt (surely with certain people you know *quicker*, quickly) but to B, when she comes home and declares happily 'I just made friends with a shop assistant at this shop' (they won't see each other again), is it best I say nothing?

Nile, famous for its impurities… Just as we're running out of strength an empty boat floats towards us. We requisition it, even though we know they'll kill us if we get caught. We sail on quietly till robbers begin chasing us. You and I are not champion rowers, let's be clear, and they close in. I shout, 'We are taking off,' and start quickly lifting myself into the sky. You hesitate a moment, then you follow me. And now we are flying in the sky except we can't keep going for much longer at this height. I see a plane at full speed and jump into it hoping you'll do the same… But you miss the turn and start plummeting. To where the robbers are waiting for us. I stick my head out the plane door and shout hysterically, 'Up!!! You need to fly UP!!!!!' I wake screaming. It's 3 a.m.

21.

The Special Monitoring Mission to Ukraine provides daily updates regarding ceasefire violations/shelling and civilian casualties/the withdrawal of weapons/armoured combat vehicles and anti-aircraft weaponry in the security zone/interrupted water supply/mines, a mine hazard sign, booby traps and unexploded ordnance (UXO).

You can read them freely online. No clearance required.

Last night I stayed at a friend's place. She had to go away and had no one to look after her boys. In the night a terrible storm started. Thunder too and vertical lightning. It was impossible to sleep and then after 3 a.m. came hail. Stas, the younger one, who is eight, said in this resigned way, 'Are we being bombed?' (the unlucky child, victim of cable TV ☺). Vlad, the ten-year-old, wasn't having a bar of it: 'If someone ordered for us to be bombed, we would have been done for by now.'

22.

U/10s soccer match, Lord Reserve, 'I am a human shield'—that's my son at centre-back, to no one in particular.

23.

I have no memory of other people being with us that day. I thought it was just you and me. Before we met you texted, 'Happy birthday. Let's

I've lost all of your letters, all photographs from before 2005. When I was moving between one place and another a bag of photo albums disap-

not see each other again.' We have form when it comes to birthdays, no?

peared. As if on purpose. As if the whole past was cut off me in one go.

24.

Jamala, "1944", 534 points. Any chance you are watching?

25.

Good morning. The pants fit me like a glove (proof's attached). Thank you a trillion, and wow!!! Classy, classic. They make—you make!—my arse look not boundless like our unvanquishable motherland but lean and elegantly bookended like Holland by Belgium & Germany.

Thank you for your New Year wishes. One slight 'but'— 'a little bit of earthly love' is not for me. I need something rare, almost magical, and not a little bit of it either.

26.

Seventy-five—my mother's age, my mother's life—years ago and I don't need to tell you how much has happened since, how many more sieges, but it's still there, not as though it happened just yesterday, but as though there

Watched everything YouTube had on it. The grip on me— physical, not just psychological. In one of the films people were fighting over a frozen sparrow that'd fallen to the ground. The 'victor' made a sparrow soup for her sick son.

could never be enough time (in the world?) to separate us from it.

27.

When the train started moving, at first slowly as if anticipating people's inability to let go of each other, you and I grabbed on to each other's clothes—do you remember?—and closed our eyes as tight as we could. And if both of us behaved as if we were drowning, it was because we *were drowning*, and now that we know how long it took us till we saw each other again I am surprised we ever let go. I had a lot of mascara on.

Day of departure... my sixteenth... yellow roses from you to me... We stuck one of the roses in the snow beside the entrance to your apartment block on Garshina, in memoriam. When the train moved I ran along the rails, in front of everyone, people seeing you off and strangers seeing strangers off. Ran screaming DON'T LEAVE. Horrible running—hysterical, frantic. Then someone brought me back to the platform and three of us ended up going to your flat to pick up records of Grebenschikov you'd left for me and a Young Scientist Chemistry Lab pack.

Somebody told me to put it on because it'd stop me crying too hard. You didn't use make-up then. Those subsequent photographs in which your face was painted always struck me as weird. You had the natural beauty even though we were taught that Jewish girls like us could be 'striking' or 'attractive' but never 'naturally beautiful'. Those Slavic girls, those human birch trees, they had it. We didn't. Except you did.

That yellow rose spent the night in the snow outside the door of your apartment block. 'Your' apartment block.

28.
I have no memory of other people that day. I know it couldn't have just been you and me.

'Immigration is your guts on the pavement. It is harakiri': we watch Dina Rubina's interview on the same day. You/me (t) here.

29.
We were best friends. I wrote about us. I wrote—thank you for not dying. But this was to you only, in private correspondence.

30.
Did you ever end up reading this?

'It rarely lends a hand
in uphill tasks,
like moving furniture,
or lifting luggage,
or going miles in shoes that pinch.

It usually steps out
whenever meat needs chopping
or forms have to be filled.'

31.

'Let me explain to you how it works. (Hello, my little
one.) Let's take a person of thirty-five and return to
her the consciousness of herself as a fifteen-year-old.
They say it's possible for that fifteen-year-old to then "remember" her life for the next twenty years. OK, this is not brilliantly
explained but did you get it? Almost? Anyway I decided I was
going to make myself twenty-five so I could "remember" my
life for the last nine years. So I went through a long corridor,
smoke everywhere, light somewhere ahead; finally, a push and
I materialised in a room (all covered in a see-through, enveloping smoke). Inside, a feeling: in a moment now I'll see everything and... You do that too, OK? See if you and I will be in
the same room again? Hey and forgive my terrible (most likely)
handwriting. Lounging on the bed. What a stupid letter this
ended up being, but it's OK, right?'

32.

Before we met you said, 'Let's not see each other again. There is no need. No point.' I said, 'Give me an hour.' I didn't mean an hour. I meant the rest of times.

ACKNOWLEDGEMENTS

In Russian we talk of the 'deepest bow' to speak of an over-whelming sense of gratitude. Head-to-toe gratitude. You can also translate it as the 'lowest bow' because you're bending forward and down as fully as you can, except in English, though not in Russian, lowest bow has slight undertones of servility.

My deepest bow is to you whose lives and worlds I write about—in a chapter, in a sentence, doesn't matter. I won't line you up here, list you all in one breathless sentence, because a few of your names have been changed or used sans surnames or fully scrubbed out to keep things safe, so my little parade won't feel right. I followed some of you around for years, read your diaries, asked you questions about the worst of times (the best of times too, I hope), we talked and talked and talked, and then I took so long to write this book that most of you, at one point or another if you still remembered this thing I was doing, were convinced it would never happen. There is a sorry there in my deepest bow.

I have had eye-opening conversations while researching this book and have tried to bring most of them into the book. I hope you, my wise guides, will recognise yourself in these pages and feel my respect and gratitude for what you have shared and shown me.

Sam Cooney, my publisher—I want to say that you and your allies and colleagues at *The Lifted Brow* and now Brow Books are the future of publishing in this country, but of course you're already the formidable present. I am thrilled to be your eldest author, so far. And big thanks to Brett Weekes for designing and typesetting this book, including over Christmas. I am probably burning bridges here (I don't mean to, as my children would say) but yours is the first book cover of mine I like.

My friends who read me: Melinda Harvey, Ellena Savage, Zoe Dzunko, Billie Tumarkin* (*daughter), Geordie Williamson who was going to be my publisher for a while there but first I was late and then you needed to get back to writing your own books—thank you in a big way for... reading me. It's the greatest service you could offer.

Thank you to my agent Clare Forster of Curtis Brown. Some writers more than other writers are dud clients (it's not like I have TV series on the go) but you have been in my corner all the way through, honest, smart, clear-headed and ready to bail me out if things get messy, and with me things get messy.

I received a Sidney Myer Creative Fellowship in 2013–14 and a Creative Victoria grant at some point too. No money=no books. Sidney Myer was a particularly incredible reprieve. Two years of not worrying about money, can you believe it?

Thank you, dear Rai Gaita—I owe so much of my ability to survive with dignity as a writer and a thinker in this world to you.

My friends Alexandra Anenska, Jessica Little, Nina Purdey, Deb Anderson, Aneta Podkalicka, Sarah O'Donnell, Katia

Margolis, Perrie Ballantine, Jen Vuk, Jo Case, Emily Potter—thank you for your friendship. What's the point of anything, and I include books here, without friends like you?

In 2016 I started work in the creative writing program at the University of Melbourne. I have never worked with a better group of people. I know that sounds vague, and like I am ticking things off some list. How about this: everyone is real and kind and gifted and funny and committed, no bullies, no predators, no passives-aggressive, no bureaucrats, people are working their arses off yet remain magnanimous and brilliantly collegial. Thank you, colleagues. Please don't let it ever change!

My dear astonishing family—thank you for bearing with me—Billie, Miguel, my parents Marian and Svetlana, and my aunt Lina. Charlie. Oh you all did so much more than bearing.

My husband (we're not married) and my editor Christian—acknowledgements tend to get soggy when writers talk about their significant others. Too intimate and smug at once, bring in the violins, I always look away when I get to this point, second-hand embarrassment is what it's called I think, not that I read other people's acknowledgements that much. Christian, the point is that you're a genius writer and a genius editor and you have given so much to me and this book that I wish (you're totally against this idea and will try to edit this line out as well, it may get ugly, a tussle...) I could put your name on the cover too. In whatever way this book floats and stumbles through the world, for me it is and will always be ours, not mine.

MARIA TUMARKIN is a writer and cultural historian. She is the author of three previous books of ideas, *Traumascapes*, *Courage*, and *Otherland*, all of which received critical acclaim in Australia, where she lives. Her most recent work, *Axiomatic*, won the 2018 Melbourne Prize for Literature's Best Writing Award.

Transit Books is a nonprofit publisher of international and American literature, based in Oakland, California. Founded in 2015, Transit Books is committed to the discovery and promotion of enduring works that carry readers across borders and communities. Visit us online to learn more about our forthcoming titles, events, and opportunities to support our mission.

TRANSITBOOKS.ORG